rowboat in a hurricane

ROWBOAT IN A

JULIE ANGUS

HURRICANE

*my amazing journey
across a changing
atlantic ocean*

GREYSTONE BOOKS
Douglas & McIntyre Publishing Group
Vancouver/Toronto/Berkeley

Greystone Books
A division of D&M Publishers Inc.
2323 Quebec Street, Suite 201
Vancouver BC Canada V5T 4S7
www.greystonebooks.com

Library and Archives Canada Cataloguing in Publication
Angus, Julie
Rowboat in a hurricane : my amazing journey across a changing
Atlantic Ocean / Julie Angus.
Includes bibliographical references and index.

ISBN 978-1-55365-337-0

1. Angus, Julie—Travel—Atlantic Ocean. 2. Atlantic Ocean—Description
and travel. 3. Boats and boating—Atlantic Ocean. 4. Marine ecology—
Atlantic Ocean. 5. Rowers—Canada—Biography. I. Title.
G530.A52A52 2008   910.4'5'092   C2008-903327-2

Editing by Susan Folkins
Cover photographs courtesy of author
except image of clouds: Gerald French/Getty Images
Text design by Naomi MacDougall

Printed and bound in Canada by Friesens
Printed on acid-free paper that is forest friendly (100% post-consumer
recycled paper) and has been processed chlorine free
Distributed in the U.S. by Publishers Group West

We gratefully acknowledge the financial support of the Canada Council for the Arts,
the British Columbia Arts Council, the Province of British Columbia through the Book
Publishing Tax Credit, and the Government of Canada through the Book Publishing
Industry Development Program (BPIDP) for our publishing activities.

TO COLIN,

my partner in life and in adventure

CONTENTS

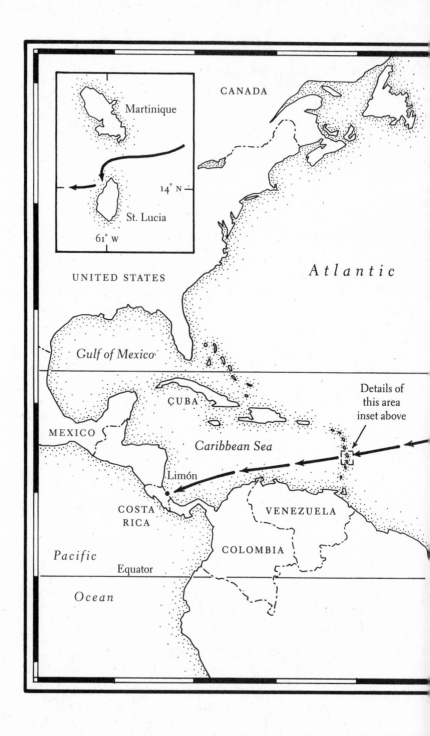

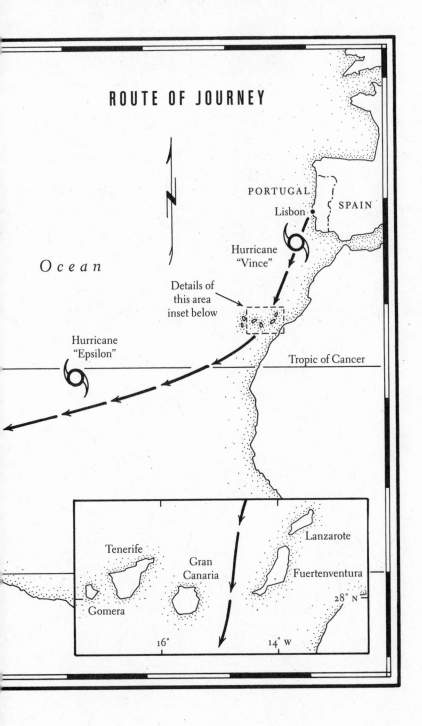

1

TAKING THE PLUNGE

WHEN I WAS eleven, my parents gave me a pet. It wasn't the dog I always wanted, but a fish—a guppy that swam between plastic fronds in its aquarium home. Glass separated us so that its watery world could exist in mine, and I used to imagine what it would be like if the situation were reversed and I existed in a fish's world.

Two decades later, in September 2005, my face was no longer pressed against aquarium glass. Instead, I watched an expansive ocean unfurl before me. I stood on a craggy cliff that was Europe's second most western point—two hours west of Lisbon, Portugal, by bike—with Colin, my husband-to-be, and together we stared at an ocean we hoped to cross in a rowboat. For the last forty-nine days we had cycled west from Russia's capital, Moscow, and finally we had reached the end of the road. In two weeks we would trade the security of land for volatile waters and begin a ten-thousand-kilometre journey across the Atlantic Ocean to North America.

More than a yearning for adventure had led me to this moment. I was drawn by the opportunity to experience the ocean from the intimate vantage offered from the deck of a rowboat. I had completed my graduate degree in molecular biology and had gone on to a career in developing therapeutics, but my personal interests now leaned towards ecology. My bookshelf sagged under the weight of volumes by Carl Safina, David Suzuki, and Sylvia Earle; it was the magnitude of the environmental issues facing our oceans that captured much of my attention. The problems of climate change, acidification, overfishing, and pollution were well documented, yet little progress was being made to solve these issues. And in a way it was easy to understand why. When I kayaked in the Gulf Islands or hiked in the Coast Mountains, I admired the Pacific Ocean for its vastness and permanence, its obliviousness to its own fragility and to the changes occurring beneath its surface. Ignoring the unseen was easy, and the very vastness of the ocean made it difficult to accept that minuscule actions on our part might have a profound impact. Through this journey I hoped to shift my understanding of the ocean to get an intimate sense of the life and dynamism that comprises it instead of viewing it as a vast, impenetrable expanse. I wanted to watch turtles as they migrated across the ocean and pelagic sharks as they hunted for tuna, to see pods of dolphins swim by and whales surface for air. I wanted to experience this environment in technicolour detail. At the same time, I wondered if I would see all the environmental perils I had read about.

NOW, WITH FORMIDABLE waves growling and slurping metres away, I began to feel nervous. My mind teemed with all the things that could go wrong—running out of food, succumbing to botulism, being attacked by sharks, encountering pirates, colliding with tankers, and contending with hurricanes and a plethora of medical emergencies. Then there was my relationship with Colin, my fiancé; he seemed like the perfect guy (which is why I said yes when he proposed), but would I still feel the same way after five months of confinement in a space the size of a closet? Would he?

It had been much easier to embrace the concept of rowing across an ocean while ensconced in the comfort of my Vancouver home. There, I could convincingly explain why moving at a turtle's pace across the sea provided unparallelled opportunities for observing the ocean, and how the months of toil would help toughen me up. But now those justifications were edged aside by a feeling of unease. As I stared across the sea, I wondered if I was making the right decision, and I struggled to distill the chain of events that had led me here.

I WISH I HAD a quick and easy answer like *It came to me in a dream* or *A fortune teller told me*, or even better, *I'm a world-class rower and I thought this would really challenge my athletic skills*.

No, my answer is more convoluted, as many things in life are. I am not an adventurer or an athlete, and I am most certainly not a rowing protégée (my first time in a rowboat was only a year earlier). In fact, for most of my life I considered the outdoors a place where unknown dangers lurked, a place best avoided. I grew up a "base brat," an only child with an air-force father and homemaker mother. We moved every four years or less and lived mostly on military bases in rented PMQs (private military quarters). My parents shunned

3

uncultivated wilderness, and they considered sports unnecessary distractions from academics that would expose their only child to wanton dangers. I grew up a timid girl whose biggest risk was a collision with a telephone pole as I walked home from school with a Stephen King novel pressed against my face.

It wasn't until the age of twenty-one, when I moved from Ontario to British Columbia for my graduate studies, that I became interested in the outdoors and athletic pursuits. I went on my first real outdoor adventure in 1998, during my inaugural spring in Victoria. A friend said, "We're going to climb Warden Peak. Do you want to come with us?"

The trip was much harder than I expected. For the first time in my life, I wore crampons, gripped an ice axe, rappelled down a sheer wall, and, while climbing that same cliff, nearly fell to what would have been a very messy landing had the belay rope not saved me. I was alternately terrified and mesmerized. For the first time I truly felt the allure of nature and the stillness of a place devoid of people. But most of the time I just thought, *Please just let me get out of here alive.* To my surprise when we emerged from the forest, the first words out of my mouth were "I can't wait to do this again."

And so the seed germinated and sprouted. It grew slowly, spindly at first and with many offshoots. I liked being in the mountains, snowboarding on groomed slopes and travelling with alpine touring skis in the backcountry. I trudged up Mount Baker, crossed its glacier while roped to a team member, and climbed its sulphurous peak. I tried rock climbing, kayaking, and surfing with little to moderate success. My repertoire of outdoor skills grew, but to be truthful, I lacked the coordination and grace that accompanies those who are athletic from a young age. I didn't really care though. I was just happy to be outside enjoying the wilderness.

When I first heard a news story on ocean rowing, I thought the rowers must be insane, bordering on suicidal. It was a sport for adrenaline junkies and lifelong athletes, not me. I couldn't row. Sharks scared me. I lived in an apartment and worked a nine-to-five job. How could I even contemplate such a journey? Yet I did, eventually. I couldn't help myself. I just kept returning to the thought—like an annoying song you can't get out of your head—of a little boat slowly crossing the ocean alongside whales and dolphins. I knew I was romanticizing it, but as these daydreams became more frequent and compelling, I couldn't stop myself from further exploring the possibility. I was hooked by the sea's wildness. Its promise of unknown adventures drew me in. As the narrator in Henry Wadsworth Longfellow's "The Secret of the Sea" says, "my soul is full of longing / For the secret of the sea, / And the heart of the great ocean / Sends a thrilling pulse through me."

So I started collecting stories on small-boat adventures and began journeying vicariously across oceans. In *Kon-Tiki*, I voyaged the Pacific Ocean with Thor Heyerdahl on a balsa wood raft. Between the pages of *Adrift*, I suffered with Steve Callahan after his boat sank and he endured seventy-six days in a life raft lost on the Atlantic. In David Shaw's book *Daring the Sea*, I rowed alongside the two Norwegian fishermen who, in 1896, became the first people to row across the Atlantic.

Between that first transatlantic rowboat voyage from New York to England and my planning in the summer of 2004, 208 additional rowers had succeeded in crossing the Atlantic Ocean. Six people had died trying, and dozens had required deep-sea rescues. The number of successful ocean crossings is low, especially when compared to other extreme endeavours such as climbing Mount Everest and skiing to the South Pole. Most oar-powered voyages connect the Canary and Caribbean islands, a distance of about 5,000 kilometres. A handful of journeys have been longer; most noteworthy are those of Sidney Genders, who in 1970 rowed 9,660 kilometres from Britain to Miami in three legs, and John Fairfax, who in 1969 rowed 8,550 kilometres from the Canary Islands to Miami. As in many extreme sports, women still tend to be a minority, but our numbers are increasing. Before I planned my attempt in 2004, eighteen women had rowed across the Atlantic Ocean. However, none had yet crossed the Atlantic from the mainland of one continent to that of another, a distance of nearly 10,000 kilometres.

The statistics told me little apart from the fact that a determined and properly outfitted individual could row across an ocean. What I really needed to know was what would be required in the way of gear, finances, knowledge, and support. Even more importantly, did I have what it would take? Was I strong enough? Was I tough enough? Would my years in an office combined with an overly protective childhood render me a physical and emotional wreck as land disappeared in the distance?

Between books and talking to people, I gained much of the theoretical knowledge needed. Hundreds of books have been written on crossing oceans in small boats. Most concern sailboats, but much of the same information applies to rowboats. I became familiar with nautical navigation, ocean dynamics, food storage, first aid, and emergency procedures. As for the mechanics of rowing, I learned that propelling an ocean rowboat is not dissimilar to propelling a common rowing shell. I practised in a friend's rowboat and later joined one of Vancouver's rowing clubs. Information specific to ocean rowing was available online, posted by others who had done similar adventures and by the British-based Ocean Rowing Society. Much of this information was related to a gruelling five-thousand-kilometre rowing race from the Canary Islands to the Caribbean, which, interestingly for me, was advertised with the catch phrase "No experience needed."

After months of wavering, I finally made the decision: *I will row across the Atlantic.* But saying these words and making the journey a reality were worlds apart.

The next crucial step would be to find a partner to do the journey with. Although many have rowed an ocean solo, doing it in tandem is more efficient, and I imagined much more enjoyable. I compiled a list of the ideal characteristics of a rowing partner and realized they were surprisingly similar to the traits I had looked for in a boyfriend. The ideal person would be calm, rational, determined, athletic, and not too insane (skeletons in the closet are a no-no when you are cooped together for months on end in a tiny boat). My fiancé, Colin, had all these traits, but I did not consider him a candidate for two reasons. I didn't want to risk losing our relationship (a disproportionate number of couples break up on sailing trips, and a rowing trip of this type would be far more stressful). Plus, he had already left on a two-year expedition and was therefore unavailable.

I told a few friends of my new plan and sought their help in my search for a partner. The idea of my journey raised a few eyebrows and led to the occasional joke about my sanity, but most of my friends were overwhelmingly supportive.

But unfortunately for me, those who had the right traits to join me in this adventure also had responsibilities or obligations that would not allow them to spend so many months away from their regular lives. I placed an advertisement on a rowing website and canvassed members of the B.C. Mountaineering Club and the Vancouver Rowing Club. Months slipped by and I was still without a partner. My friend and coworker Mary Hearnden was so determined for me to succeed that she shyly admitted, "If you can't find anyone, I'll go with you," even though her passion was the mountains and not the sea. Through Mary, though, on two multi-day treks in the mountains of Manning and Garibaldi parks she organized, I found the ideal partner: Cathy Choinicki.

Cathy loves outdoor adventure, and that passion has taken her to remote areas around the world. When we met she was in her mid-thirties and working for Environment Canada, which afforded her enough flexibility for travelling, mountaineering, and her latest pursuit: sailing. She listened to my plans with rapt enthusiasm, and when I finally asked her if she would like to join me, she said yes.

I was euphoric that my ocean row was no longer a solo affair, that I would have someone to keep me company on the sea and to share the workload of preparing for the adventure. It seemed things were slowly coming together.

Our planned departure date was eleven months away, and within that time we had two tasks: to learn how to row and to raise one hundred thousand dollars to buy a boat and cover additional costs. Learning to row was the easy part. We trained daily, often at the Vancouver Rowing Club, which sponsored us with free lessons and offered us the guidance of one of their coaches, Alex Binkley. We made marked improvements physically, but our fundraising efforts weren't following the same course. We created a website and a comprehensive sponsorship proposal package. Cathy's good friend John Rocha, the marketing director for the Vancouver Canucks hockey team, guided us in our efforts. Other experts in marketing and sponsorship generously offered advice, and a team of professionals created a powerful promotional video for us. We sent our sponsorship package to hundreds of companies and placed dozens of cold calls. Months slipped by with little sponsorship success, until finally it seemed the only way to make our expedition a reality would be to ask the banks for a loan.

By this time, Cathy was growing increasingly uninterested. Then, in mid-spring 2005, seven months before our departure date, she told me the disappointing, but not entirely surprising, news. She would not be rowing across the Atlantic with me. Cathy was concerned about the financial and health risks. She did not want to borrow huge sums of money for such an uncertain venture, and she was worried that an old shoulder injury would be further damaged by many months of constant rowing. I was devastated by such a significant step backwards, but grateful that she had truthfully assessed her commitment now instead of later. Things would have been much worse if she had given me this news just weeks or days before the journey began.

Crossing the ocean solo had some appeal, and I pondered this new reality. Other potential partners also came to mind. While Cathy and I had been training and planning, several people had expressed interest in rowing across an ocean. In particular, the father of one of my best friends, a sixty-five-year-old Scot with a passion for rowing, seemed an excellent candidate. Liz, his daughter, proudly lobbied on her father's behalf: "My dad could do it. He used to be the top rower in his class and he's still got it." Then she added, "As long as you bring enough rum, he'll be fine." I could imagine ocean parties with her father singing sea shanties as we rowed and drank our way across the Atlantic.

Really, though, things weren't looking good for my proposed adventure. I had raised absolutely no money, I might have to partner with a senior citizen, and I hadn't even bought a boat yet.

As it turned out, I was not the only one with expedition problems. A few weeks earlier, Colin had called me from the chilled depths of Siberia on an Iridium satellite telephone to deliver some unsettling news.

"Hi, baby, it's me," he said. His voice was clear but fractionally delayed because of the thousands of kilometres between us.

"Honey, how are you? Is everything all right?" I asked.

"Yeah, I guess so. The only thing is I'm on my own now. Tim and I are taking some time apart and are going to cycle independently to Irkutsk."

I worried about Colin travelling alone through Siberia. The city of Irkutsk was several thousand kilometres away. Temperatures were still twenty to thirty degrees below zero, and he was cycling on extremely remote roads. I imagined him alone, struggling through a frozen region vaster than all of Canada, and shivered.

"Do you really think that's a good idea?" I asked.

"Don't worry," Colin assured me, "the people around here are friendly and the temperatures are starting to warm up. Things just aren't working out with Tim and me. I need a break. Hopefully we'll be able to continue together from Irkutsk."

After we finished chatting, I couldn't stop thinking about my boyfriend struggling all alone through Siberia. What if he was mugged or got hit by a truck? Who would contact me? Would it just be a long, endless silence lacking punctuation? I thought back to when Colin had slipped a ring on my finger several weeks before the expedition, asking me if I would marry him. A tear dropped onto the handset that I was still absent-mindedly hanging onto.

Colin had been on several expeditions before this, including rafting both the Amazon and Yenisey rivers from source to sea, as well as extensive offshore sailing adventures. And for as long as I had known him, he had spent every moment preparing for this journey. For more than a decade, it had been his dream to circumnavigate the world entirely by human power—a 42,000-kilometre journey through seventeen countries that would take an estimated two years. For the last three years, he'd been working full-time on making it a reality. I had helped him prepare and when he began the expedition I continued assisting him with website updates, equipment needs, and route research. Being so closely involved in his expedition had helped me hone many of the skills needed to prepare for my own journey across the Atlantic, and undoubtedly further fuelled my own longing for adventure.

Colin had also had problems finding a suitable partner and, in the end, chose someone he did not know well. He and Tim had completed 8,000 kilometres of their 42,000-kilometre journey together, but they still had a long way to go. Almost a year before, I had left Vancouver with them, cycling to Hyder, Alaska, before returning to my Vancouver job, while they continued by bike to Whitehorse, Yukon. They then followed the Yukon River by canoe to Fairbanks, Alaska. In Fairbanks, they continued down the rest of the river to the Bering Sea in a specially designed rowboat, and then rowed across the North Pacific to Siberia. Bicycles, skis, and their feet had taken them across Siberia, first together and, now that the conditions were slightly less formidable, separately.

Up to this point, Colin and Tim had focussed all their time, resources, and research on the first half of their expedition—the journey from Vancouver to Moscow. The second, and more difficult, leg of their expedition was still in the infancy stages of planning. The scant sponsorship dollars they had raised had long been spent and Colin had gone through tens of thousands of dollars in personal savings—his bank account was near zero. He didn't have enough money to buy a rowboat for himself and Tim or time to look for sponsors. Now there was the very real possibility that Tim and Colin would not be able to reconcile, and that Colin would be travelling solo unless he found another travel partner. It was another wrench thrown into a very difficult expedition.

When Cathy told me her decision, I wondered if perhaps this was a fateful sign. I decided to refrain from recruiting any rum-toting Scotsmen for the time being. If Colin and Tim didn't patch things up, Colin might need to partner with someone else to cross the Atlantic Ocean. I knew this could place undo strain on our relationship, but at the same time, deep inside I couldn't imagine anyone I would rather share this unique adventure with.

A month later I received an e-mail from Colin, who was now in the southern Siberian city of Irkutsk. He and Tim hadn't reunited, and their relations had become increasingly acrimonious via cyber-communication. Colin finally told Tim that they simply couldn't continue together and proposed that they carry on travelling independently and reunite just before Vancouver. It was in no one's interest for this expedition to turn into a competition.

While Colin was in Irkutsk, we communicated almost exclusively by e-mail because of the expense and complications of using local telephones. Messages flew back and forth as we discussed the possibility of attempting an Atlantic row together. Our big concern was what it could do to our relationship. In civilization we got along wonderfully, but what would happen when we were cooped together for months in a rowboat? The deterioration of Colin and Tim's friendship in the field was an example that could not be overlooked. We didn't want to jeopardize our strong relationship at any cost. Ultimately, after much back-and-forth, we decided our relationship would withstand the added stresses of an extended ocean row.

I would join Colin in Moscow and we would cycle 5,000 kilometres through Europe to Lisbon, Portugal. From here we would row across the Atlantic Ocean to North America—most likely Miami—before cycling back to Vancouver. It was an abrupt change from my initial plan of rowing from the Canary Islands to the Caribbean, a 5,000-kilometre journey. Now I would attempt a 10,000-kilometre row from mainland to mainland, and be the first woman to do so. Just a few casual e-mails had more than quadrupled the overall length of my journey to a 23,000-kilometre odyssey.

I felt a little uneasy. It had been hard enough wrapping my mind around a 5,000-kilometre voyage to the tropics. Now, not only was the row itself twice the distance, but I would be travelling more than halfway around the planet using just a bicycle and a rowboat.

By late May, one month before my departure for Moscow, many daunting tasks remained undone. Since Colin was on the road, I was taking care of pretty much all the logistics for the Atlantic row. Financially things still looked dismal. Colin had exhausted all his savings, and I was still unable to get any financial sponsorship. I had only one month to raise tens of thousands of dollars, purchase a rowboat, and tend to the litany of chores required to row across an ocean. The task of preparing for the ocean row was so great that I didn't expect to have more than a weekend to plan for our bike ride across Europe. And that was only if I worked full-time on expedition planning, but I also had a day job.

Since finishing my master's degree in molecular biology five years before, I had worked in the biotechnology industry. Recently, though, I had made a major career change, leaving my job in biotech to work as a consultant. But when I expanded my endeavour from rowing five thousand kilometres across the Atlantic, which would take three months, to rowing twice that distance and cycling another thirteen thousand kilometres from Moscow to Vancouver, which would take a year, I had effectively put my career on hold. I shifted my efforts entirely to expedition preparations. The next few weeks were a whirlwind of activities—finding an appropriate boat, researching the weather patterns for the Atlantic Ocean, ordering a miscellaneous array of required equipment, and continuing the fruitless search for funds.

NOW, SEVERAL MONTHS later, as I gazed at the deep blue ocean from the shores of Portugal, the intense preparations leading up to this moment came back to me in a blur. My mind had been perpetually occupied with logistics, financial troubles, and worries about Colin's safety. Even after we had united in Moscow I had been overwhelmed with the labour of cycling twelve hours a day, filming our journey, and continuing to coordinate Atlantic logistics from roadside phone booths. Up until this point, I had been so busy getting everything ready that I had little time to ponder the reality of living in a rowboat on a vast ocean.

Cycling across a continent had been an intimidating challenge for a computer-addled, office-bound molecular biologist. Now, with salt spray misting my face and endless blue in front of me, the enormity of the upcoming voyage began to terrify me.

2

ROWBOAT PREPARATIONS
IN LISBON

THE NEXT MORNING we went to the marina to wait for the truck that was delivering our rowboat from the northern tip of Scotland.

I had found the rowboat—a six-year-old boat made specifically for rowing on oceans—for sale on the Internet. The style, a Woodvale Pairs class boat, was designed by two British boat-builders in 1995, and had since proven to be the most popular style of ocean rowboat. It was made from quarter-inch plywood and epoxy—an ideal combination of materials that made the boat both lightweight and relatively strong (the whole boat weighed about 350 kilograms empty and 800 kilograms fully loaded).

The rowboat was just over seven metres, only slightly longer than a two-person ocean kayak, although considerably beamier and deeper. It had two tiny cabins. The forward one (no bigger than a kitchen cupboard) would be for storage, and the aft cabin (about the size of a small closet) would become our living quarters. Sandwiched between the two cabins was an open deck containing two sliding rowing seats positioned in tandem. The below-deck space was divided into many sealed compartments, the rationale being that if one compartment was holed by hitting a reef or an iceberg, the flooding would not spread throughout the boat. I found this comforting until I realized the *Titanic* had had the same feature. Designed with similar principles to a lifeboat, the Woodvale Pairs boat is also self-righting. Theoretically it can endure horrific weather, flip end-over-end, and still remain afloat.

At Doca de Belém, we reserved a spot for our boat in the marina's dry-dock compound, and booked their crane to unload our boat.

"I can't believe the boat is finally arriving," Colin said, a wide grin plastered on his face, as we emerged from the manager's office.

It was a huge relief. The boat had been late because of problems with the freight company. But now the Portuguese truck driver rolled back a section of the truck's roof and unfastened the strapping that secured the boat. A staff member from the marina manoeuvred the yard crane over the truck. The driver slipped two canvas straps under the boat and trailer, and with one fluid motion the unit was transferred out of the truck and onto the concrete pier.

"Maybe you two are a little crazy," the rotund driver said, "but you have guts." He clapped me on the back. "My wife and children will not believe me when I tell them what you are doing." At least that's what I think he said. He was speaking Portuguese, and I could make out only "crazy" and "wife."

Once the truck was gone, Colin and I cheerfully pushed the trailer and boat to the spot we had rented in the dry-dock compound.

"You've picked a great boat," Colin beamed, as he explored the interior of the vessel. "It's well constructed. Good attention to detail. See these hatches? They're British-made and top of the line. When I was on my sailboat, I could only dream of equipment like this."

"It was built by professionals," I said. "The survey showed no structural problems, but there are a few things that need work."

"No problem, we can do it," Colin said.

GETTING AN OCEAN rowboat ready for a crossing is a challenging affair. From the research I had done in Vancouver, I learned that preparing for an ocean row usually takes two years and a quarter of a million dollars. And that is for voyages half as long as ours. We had two weeks and dwindling credit limits.

Colin and I left our cheap hotel and moved into a vacant shop at the marina, where the manager kindly allowed us to stay for free. Our new concrete abode became our temporary expedition headquarters, allowing us to store and organize our growing pile of equipment and supplies. Best of all, being a stone's throw from our vessel allowed us to work from dawn until bedtime on repairs.

We unpacked and inventoried the equipment that had come with the boat: sea anchors, harnesses, a desalination unit, solar panels, and a VHF radio, among other things. Many of the products in the first aid kit had expired or were of dubious integrity, but we found a few useful items, such as shark repellent powder and sutures.

When I had travelled to the north of Scotland to test the rowboat before buying it, I had left a duffle bag full of expedition equipment in the boat. But now, as I peered inside the bag, my heart sank.

"My fleece jacket is gone," I said with surprise. "So are our rowing gloves, and the Helly Hansen marine shoes. Even the lamb's wool I packed for making seat covers is missing, and the Santa hat to celebrate Christmas."

"At least we have our rowboat," Colin said, trying to console me.

I searched the cabin frantically for the most valuable item I had left on board. Sure enough, my laptop computer was gone. We had planned to use it to send out website updates, communicate with the media, get weather forecasts, and track our GPS position so that people always knew where we were.

"I can imagine why someone would steal a computer, but Christmas decorations and rowing equipment?" Colin said.

There was not much we could do; we didn't have money to buy another computer, and it was still too early in the season to buy new Christmas decorations.

BEFORE WE DID anything, we made lists—endless to-do lists of chores and equipment. Not only did we need to purchase all the tools and items to repair our boat, but we needed to pack our vessel with every item required for an unsupported three-to-five month journey.

Lisbon, with three marine stores conveniently located near the marina, is well suited to boaters. We became regular customers at each one. We peppered the staff with endless questions. "Can you order a connector cable for our radio?" "Do you sell GPS units?" "Where can we get a diaphragm for our bilge pump?" "When will the antifouling paint come in?" "Where can I find eighty litres of rubbing alcohol for my cookstove?"

At the hardware shops, we filled several shopping carts with fibreglass, resin, screwdrivers, hammers, sandpaper, buckets, and paint. We made so many unusual purchases—at least for tourists—that both our credit cards were automatically suspended multiple times for suspicious activity.

Finally, with a respectable set of the most affordable hand tools we could find, we set about repairing the boat. We scrubbed every inch, inside and out, with soap and steel wool, removing several years of grime and paint in an advanced stage of peeling. We repaired damaged areas with fibreglass strips and polyester resin. We fixed leaky hatches and rebuilt the defunct desalination unit. Beneath the water line we brushed antifouling paint that would supposedly keep our boat free of barnacles, seaweed, and other growth. We sanded and painted the rest of the boat red and white in the colours of the Canadian flag. We even created the outline of the maple leaf using masking tape and red paint. We then used vinyl lettering to display our website address and the boat's name, *Ondine*. The name was a tribute to Colin's first boat, an eight-metre sailboat he bought as a teenager and in which he spent five years exploring the South Pacific.

WHILE WE READIED our boat, Mother Nature graced us with perfect weather. Ocean breezes cooled us while the sun shone from a cloudless sky. Ornamental palms around the dry-dock compound rustled but rarely swayed. Children piloted tiny Sabot sailboats in the water below, while barges and freighters navigated the depths farther out. Though we rushed to and fro, only breaking for quick meals, we appreciated our idyllic, sleepy backdrop. This late summer reverie wasn't going to last, though. The arrival of fall would inevitably bring degrading weather and heavy southwesterly winds.

We had studied several marine pilot books and were well versed in the prevailing weather patterns. From about April until mid- to late September, the weather off the Portuguese coast is at its best. During this period, the Portuguese trade winds—gentle south-moving winds and currents—create a situation that would be ideal for taking us to the lower latitudes, where we would continue to encounter favourable conditions. From October to March, the weather becomes less stable, and heavy winds from the west and southwest are frequent. Sustained winds from the west would probably overpower our rowing efforts, and our plywood vessel could be wrecked along the numerous cliffs adorning Portugal's coast. We had to depart before the Portuguese trade winds faltered. It was now already September 15, however—the date we had hoped to leave by. Although things were moving forward steadily, we still had a lot of work to do.

Even if we could travel across the ocean during the ideal time window, we based our weather predictions on recent historical records, and there were signs that change was afoot. Three weeks earlier, Hurricane Katrina had decimated New Orleans. It was the sixth-strongest Atlantic hurricane ever recorded, a category-five hurricane on the Saffir-Simpson scale. According to *The Federal Response to Hurricane Katrina*, a White House report issued in February 2006, 1,330 people died in the storm, another 2,096 people were still missing five months later, and US$96 billion in damages was caused, making it the costliest hurricane in history. At the time it occurred, we were shocked, not only by the devastation and loss of life, but by what was shaping up to be a very bad hurricane season. Katrina was the eleventh named storm—the average is ten—and the second category-five hurricane that year. Category-five hurricanes occur only about once every three years; only in two other years, 1960 and 1961, did two category-five hurricanes form. We were troubled by this, but even worse, we were only halfway through the hurricane season, and we had no idea what the next three months would hold.

Compared to their predecessors, today's hurricanes are like steroid-enhanced bodybuilders. The same month that Katrina flexed her muscles, a scientific report in the journal *Nature* by Massachusetts Institute of Technology meteorology professor Kerry Emanuel, one of *Time* magazine's one hundred most influential people, showed that the power of hurricanes has increased nearly 70 per cent since the 1970s. Storms are more intense and last longer. The once-rare monsters, category-four and -five hurricanes with wind speeds over 210 kilometres per hour, are increasingly common; their numbers have doubled in the last thirty-five years. And hurricanes are not only increasing in intensity. In a July 2007 study published by the Royal Society of London, researchers concluded that there are twice as many Atlantic hurricanes now compared to one hundred years ago.

The big question, of course, is why. A number of scientists suggest that climate change has played a role. Elevated ocean temperatures and the related increase in humidity (warm air holds more moisture) caused by global warming both increase hurricane intensity and duration. In the last thirty years, ocean surface temperatures have jumped 0.5 degrees Celsius. Seawater captures heat from the air, which settles not only into the surface waters (the top 30 metres) where temperatures of at least 26.5 degrees Celsius are needed for hurricanes to form, but as deep as 450 metres. Because of this increase in heat at such depths, less cool water is available to come to the surface and stop a hurricane's growth.

I hoped this expedition would help me to better understand the environmental challenges the ocean was facing, but the heightened risk of encountering a hurricane was not something I had prepared for.

ALTHOUGH WEATHER WAS our biggest worry, Portuguese bureaucracy placed a close second. We'd ordered equipment from overseas—three-metre oars from Australia, freeze-dried foods from the U.S., electronic gear from Canada—and we struggled to retrieve it. We knew we could not buy these items in Portugal, so we had them shipped there while we cycled across Europe. Even that wasn't easy because we didn't have anyone in Lisbon to accept our parcels. General delivery at the post office wouldn't work because many items were being shipped by courier. The Canadian Embassy in Lisbon flatly refused to accept anything on our behalf. Eventually, we found a hotel that would accept our packages and, after a longer search, we found Mario Almeida, a friend of a friend who lives in Lisbon, who would do the same.

"You must come to the airport to pick them up," the shipping clerk said when the carbon-fibre oars donated to us by the Australian company Croker Oars arrived. We were thrilled that they had made it to Portugal safely. However, it took eight hours in four separate offices to complete the required customs paperwork. Two kind women from the shipping company patiently spent the day with us, walking from office to office, translating, and handing us documents to sign. They even organized a meeting with the manager so that our import duty was waived. And despite no import duty or shipping, it still cost us four hundred euros in administrative fees to retrieve the oars.

We soon learned that the procedure was different for each package that arrived, and that the oars had been the easiest to retrieve. We spent countless hours on the phone with each courier company, muddling through a minefield of bureaucracy. Sometimes we were told, "You can only receive packages in Portugal if you are a Portuguese citizen." Mario, our new Portuguese friend, came to the rescue and claimed they were his. Slowly, we ticked essential items off the list: a GPS, navigational charts, underwater camera housings, a life raft, an emergency beacon (EPIRB), and various other odds and ends. But by our new hoped-for departure date, September 20, we still hadn't been able to wrest all our packages free from Portuguese customs. Boxes of freeze-dried food, sent from North America by sponsor Mountain House Foods, were still being withheld from us.

We could not find freeze-dried foods in Lisbon, so we had no choice but to outfit our boat with food from the supermarket. Freeze-dried food is lightweight, nutritious, and easy to prepare—ideal for a long journey where every ounce of weight matters. But instead we'd have to rely on heavier and more difficult-to-prepare ingredients available in local grocery stores. Also, since we didn't have a refrigerator, we'd have to be careful to select items that could weather the tropical heat. We'd have to stow enough food to last the two of us for up to five months. It would barely fit in the boat.

We arrived at the wholesale supermarket Makro armed with a shopping list, or perhaps more accurately a shopping *book*. After mulling over our nutritional requirements, we'd done our best to itemize what would be required to get us across the ocean in good health. For breakfast we would rotate among four meals: rice pudding, tapioca pudding, cream of wheat, and oatmeal. Lunches would be dried bread with peanut butter, tuna, preserved meat, or cheese (while it lasted). Our planned dinners offered the most variety; each meal contained a carbohydrate (noodles, rice, mashed potatoes, and couscous), a protein (tuna, canned meat, beans), and, every other day, a can of vegetables. For snacks we decided on daily rations of half a pound of cookies, a handful of dried fruit, and five candies. Our goal was to bring foods that were easy to prepare, lightweight, dense, nutritious, and calorie-loaded. We each needed to eat about five thousand calories a day, about twice as much as we'd consume normally.

Colin pushed the cart through the aisles while I read off our shopping list. "We need 130 cans of tuna, 60 cans of beans, 35 kilograms of rice . . . Is 100 litres of powdered milk enough, or should I get two sacks? . . . These vegetables are too expensive; do we really need that many cans? . . . I think we should get extra candy instead of canned fruit, it's cheaper . . . Should we get ten flats of Oreo cookies, or do you want some oatmeal crisps too?"

We spent hours wandering the supermarket aisles and were finally ready to check out with an obscene amount of food. Imagine a week's total groceries for a typical person and multiply that by eighty (we were shopping for two for twenty weeks at double the caloric intake). The clerk's eyes opened wide as we dragged one heavy cart after another up to the till. After almost an hour of scanning, the clerk finally gestured to the shocking figure displayed on the screen.

"I'll pay by credit card," I said, handing over my MasterCard.

A long queue had formed behind us, and the clerk's expression transformed from shock to dismay. "We don't accept credit cards. It's cash only."

We had become the centre of attention. Members of management had gathered around the perimeter of our shopping carts to see what was going on. Passing shoppers would momentarily pause, wearing the same guilty expressions as those going out of their way to view a gruesome car accident. I felt these nightmarish situations were becoming all too familiar.

"Uh . . . we didn't know that . . . I guess we'll go to the bank machine and come back in few minutes," Colin said.

We walked hurriedly out the door, leaving the staff scratching their heads.

"Let's just leave. We can't get that kind of money from the ATM," Colin said.

"We can't just go. We spent the entire day collecting that food. We've got to get the money somehow," I said, shocked at the prospect of just walking away.

"Well, the banks will be closed until Monday. What else can we do?" Colin argued.

"My bank at home is open on Saturday. Maybe I can call them and see if they can temporarily increase my ATM limit and place some money in my account from my credit card," I said doubtfully.

It seemed a very unlikely possibility, but it was our only chance. I went to a public phone and made the call. Ten minutes later I received the news that they would do it. After a quick trip to the ATM, we returned to the cashier, our pockets bulging with euros. The patient, kind manager then offered to deliver our food to the marina to save us from having to hire a fleet of taxis.

Finally, on September 21, just over two weeks after our arrival in Lisbon, we had our boat shipshape and packed with everything needed for the long journey across the ocean. The last two weeks we'd worked nonstop, from 5:30 AM to 11:30 PM, but somehow we had managed to transform an empty secondhand rowboat into one that was completely seaworthy and equipped with all the essential gear required to row across an ocean. We triple-tested all our equipment and had backups for all the critical gear, such as the desalinator and Iridium satellite phone, not to mention repair materials to deal with practically every emergency scenario. We had stocks of wholesome food, and even some fishing gear, just in case we wanted to fish en route. More than a few times, I had thought we might not be able to prepare our boat in time, but now we were ready to go.

3

LEAVING LAND

"RISE AND SHINE. High tide is two hours away," I said, nudging Colin in the side with my elbow.

He issued the expected response: a dissatisfied grunt. It was 4:00 AM on Thursday, September 22. We'd had only three hours of sleep, and now we were embarking on a ten-thousand-kilometre row across the Atlantic.

We extracted ourselves from the snug rowboat cabin and began the final preparations for departure. We needed to leave with the outgoing tide, which was in three hours; otherwise we'd have to wait another day. Our boat was now in the water, tied to a pontoon at Doca de Belém, which was located on a two-kilometre-wide channel on the estuary of Portugal's main river. The Tagus boasted currents so strong that they changed the geography of the river to form a partially inverted delta. The raised triangle of sediment that usually collects at a river's mouth was absent. Now the incoming current—intensified by strong tides that accompanied the nearly full moon—was still close to its peak power; it would be impossible to row against. Within a few hours, however, this great force would work in our favour.

After storing the last of the food, repacking gear to make it fit in the cramped compartments, and filling water containers, we were ready to go. At least I hoped so. I was both terrified and thrilled that our trip was finally underway. We were setting off only a few days later than the target date we had set months ago. It was tempting to postpone our departure another day so that we could give the boat one more inspection and get a good night's sleep, but we worried that the stable weather would soon deteriorate. The sooner we travelled south, the better.

"I can't shake the feeling that we're forgetting something," I said.

"I've got the list here, and we've checked everything off," Colin replied.

"It's too bad we can't get delivery on the ocean," I joked. "It'd be great if we could call up a Lisbon restaurant and have them bring us a few meals of grilled fish and veggies."

"Wouldn't that be nice," Colin laughed. "And we could be teleported to a soft bed every night."

Our light banter only further emphasized the spartan existence we would soon be facing. A few hundred metres from our boat, cars and trains whizzed along the waterfront as Lisbon's work force prepared for another day. Behind the busy street, old stone architecture stood bathed in city lights, and a predawn glow hinted at the city's permanence. Only a few days before, I had been longing to escape this hectic world of noise, dust, and machines. Now I wasn't so sure. In the other direction, towards the open Atlantic, the water absorbed and diffused what little light there was, creating a thick grey mat. I felt I was looking into a chasm of nothingness, a world yet to be created.

Once we pushed off from the dock, our world would be restricted to the space between the gunwales of our small plywood boat. Forgetting something that might normally be inconsequential, such as sunscreen lotion or a can opener, could lead to devastating consequences. So could many other things, such as miscalculating the amount of fuel we'd need for the stove, not bringing enough batteries for the backup GPS, or forgetting a crucial tool. The list of considerations was seemingly infinite. We had realized we must be able to remedy any problem that might occur—from a snapped oar to a broken bone. Self-sufficiency was paramount to survival.

"Wow, that is one packed boat," Colin said, as he stood on the dock surveying the vessel.

He was right. The gear that we couldn't fit in the storage compartments was lashed onto the deck or squeezed into the cabin. The sleeping berth, designed to be just wide enough for two people, was crowded with supplies that should have been stored elsewhere. Not only did our home look like a cross between a kayak and a dishevelled miniature house-boat, it also sat precariously low in the water because of this excess weight. The scuppers—openings on the sides of the boat that normally allow water on the decks to drain—sat barely above the water line. On the open ocean, the vessel would be sluggish and prone to waves sluicing over the decks. As we ate our way through the cargo, however, the boat would gradually become more manageable. Like a rocket heading into space, it would become faster and more manoeuvrable as fuel was consumed.

A shadowy cluster of five people huddled on the dock to see us off. Two sailors from yachts moored nearby joined Mario, his wife, and another friend. Although it was barely 7:00 AM, they had forsaken the warmth of their beds to bid us farewell. They offered parting gifts and words of wisdom, hugs and promises to stay in touch, plus one bottle of wine "to celebrate your birthdays," another "to bring in the New Year," and a third "to mark the halfway point." I happily stowed the additional cargo despite our weight concerns, thinking we'd drink all the wine within the first week.

We untied our rowboat, stowed the fenders, and pushed off from our berth. Colin steered us through rows of sailboats while I waved goodbye to our friends, to Lisbon, and to life on land. Within minutes we reached the main channel of the Tagus, and its strong tidal current doubled our speed to four knots, swiftly moving us away from the marina. Lisbon's striking April 25 Bridge spanned the channel a few kilometres upstream and slipped into the distance. This long red suspension bridge reminded me of San Francisco's Golden Gate Bridge, which I later found out is its sister bridge. Built in 1962, it was later renamed to commemorate the day in 1974 that the Carnation Revolution—a two-year movement that replaced Europe's longest dictatorship with a liberal democracy and culminated with crowds of Portuguese walking the streets, holding red carnations for peace—began.

Further down the channel towered the seventeen-storey concrete prow of a fifteenth-century sailboat called *Monument to the Discoveries*. Its deck was lined with illustrations of thirty famous Portuguese explorers from centuries ago; it was another reminder of the pivotal role Portugal played in mapping (and ruling) the world during the Age of Discovery.

It was hard to believe that a country one-tenth the size of British Columbia was the first global empire, claiming territories that included Africa, South America, and Asia, but seafaring prowess had been its advantage.

So many monumental voyages of exploration had commenced from this very harbour, and I felt like we were embarking on our own journey of discovery. When Colin tired on the oars, we switched positions and I pulled the blades through the water in long, steady strokes. The sun was now shining from a clear sky, and the anxiety I had felt a few hours earlier was lifting.

"We're at 4.5 knots!" I said, glancing at the GPS.

"Wow! Those rowing lessons you took are really paying off," Colin said as he fiddled with a rope securing the life raft. "See if you can get 5."

I pulled even harder on the lightweight oars, but was soon distracted by another famous Lisbon landmark, the Tower of Belém. This sixteenth-century white castle looks far too ornate to protect the city of Belém from invading forces as it once did. Although it is fortified and the windows are small, delicate carvings encircle the balconies and watchtowers.

It took little imagination to envision those great ships of the past leaving this harbour, and the crew's conflicting feelings of excitement and trepidation. They had headed out to great discoveries and equally momentous dangers—scurvy, mutiny, and warring attacks to name a few. The sailors had left port knowing that they might not return to their mothers, wives, or children. As Laurence Bergreen writes in his book *Over the Edge of the World*, which details the circumnavigation led by Ferdinand Magellan, "going to sea was the most dangerous thing one could do, the Renaissance equivalent of becoming an astronaut." Five vessels and a crew of 270 had left on that voyage, but after three years of unimaginable hardship, only 18 people and one ship returned to Spain. Magellan himself was killed in the Philippines.

The minds of these explorers were haunted by more than real horrors. Many believed they would boil to death if they crossed the equator, sail off the edge of the Earth, or be stalked by sea monsters that lurked in the ocean's depths. At that time, much of Europe's understanding of the world came from *Naturalis Historia*, a 1,500-year-old encyclopedia by Pliny the Elder that described the mythical horrors they would face: one-and-a-half-metre lobsters, ninety-metre eels, and tribes of cyclopean people.

Five hundred years ago, geographical knowledge was a world apart from the intricate maps and GPS systems at our disposal. Europeans knew of only three continents, Europe, Asia, and Africa, although they suspected others existed. Mediaeval maps depicted these three continents separated by two rivers (the Nile and the Don) and the Mediterranean, which all flowed into the Great Ocean Sea. Jerusalem was at the centre of the map and Paradise at the top.

As we neared the end of the channel and the exposed waters of the Atlantic, the greater concentration of salt increased the water's density and seemed to lift our boat fractionally higher. We spotted a handful of fishing boats and what appeared to be a patrol ship in the distance. As the high-powered grey vessel neared, we realized it was heading straight for us. The throaty diesel eased to a tiger's purr as the ship stopped several feet from our port gunwale. Men in fatigues placed large plastic bumpers against their boat's hull and threw us a rope. I caught the thick burlap line, looped it through a hand grip and secured it with a bowline knot.

"Where are you travelling?" asked the captain in perfect English.

"Florida," I replied.

His eyes widened fractionally.

These Portuguese patrolmen (army, police, or navy—we still weren't sure) undoubtedly had the authority to stop us from leaving. They could tow us back to land and banish us from re-entering their waters; it all hinged on how they perceived our proposed voyage. I thought of the culmination of backbreaking labour, money, and stresses that had brought us to the present moment, all of it in vain if they turned us around. I silently beseeched him to release us—perhaps with a warm laugh and happy wishes—while Colin fidgeted uncomfortably and the men began talking among themselves in Portuguese.

We had gone to great lengths to ensure that we departed from Portugal legally, within the rules delineated by customs, immigration, and the harbour police. A few days earlier, we had asked the marine police about departure protocol and whether we needed to clear anything with customs and immigration. The official had told us no; since Portugal had joined the European Union, yacht entrance and clearance formalities had eased. All that was required was the receipt for marina moorage, which would also serve as sufficient documentation for proof of stay when we entered the next country. However, we had purposely failed to mention to the official that our small vessel was a rowboat, and now that we found ourselves tied to a Portuguese law-enforcement boat on the dawn of our departure, I felt a little uneasy.

"Papers, please," the captain finally said in English.

What papers? I thought we didn't need papers? I removed our passports and the marina receipt from a waterproof bag and handed them up to the captain, hoping that was all he meant. He perused the passport pages and shifted his scrutinizing gaze to our faces. Apparently satisfied with the resemblance, he nodded and passed our materials to an officer who began a VHF radio dispatch to his supervisors.

We handed the other officers a book of news clippings on our journey, hoping that it would convey our experience and preparedness. But it was hard to gauge the response. The officers chatted animatedly to one another. Occasionally one of them would gesture to our boat with a shake of his head or a burst of laugher.

After what seemed like an eternity, the captain returned our passports to us. He smiled and said, "You are free to continue. We wish you good luck."

I breathed a sigh of relief. The last official hurdle was behind us. Ferdinand Magellan was long gone, but his nation still embraced the spirit of exploration. From now on, it was just Colin, me, and many kilometres of open sea.

4

OUR FIRST DAY
AT SEA

WHILE COLIN RESUMED rowing, I attempted to restyle our home from an overstuffed closet to something a little more livable. Too many things remained unpacked; they'd been hurriedly stuffed into wall-mounted mesh pockets instead of being neatly stored in hidden compartments. The floor of our cabin was blanketed with a three-inch closed-cell-foam mattress and, of course, this space was to be not only our bedroom, but also our kitchen, living room, office, and occasionally (when storms prevented us from exiting the cabin), our bathroom. To reach the storage areas, I moved the cabin's contents to one side, pried back the mattress, and lifted one of the plywood lids. Using my head to prop the mattress up, I crouched over the compartment and laboriously rearranged objects until I could squeeze in a few more errant items.

A gentle swell rocked the boat, and I was pleased that my stomach remained settled. Before we left, I'd been terrified

of being incapacitated by seasickness. As a child, I had suffered horrific bouts of carsickness, and even as an adult, I
often feel nauseous as a passenger on winding mountain
roads. I knew that the success of this expedition mainly
came down to mental endurance. Coping with monotony,
isolation, tedium, and fear was something I had some control over. Seasickness, on the other hand, is a physical condition that no amount of determination can quell. Over time,
severe seasickness can lead to physical deterioration, fatigue,
dehydration, and possibly even death. I had never been on
the open ocean before, and could only hope motion sickness
wouldn't strike me down.

Suddenly the state of the ocean began to change. We had
emerged from the shelter of Cabo da Roca—the westernmost
tip of Europe—and huge, slow-moving swells began to rock
our boat. I stopped packing gear and stuck my head out the
cabin door, inhaling deeply.

"Are you all right?" Colin asked.

No, of course not. Look at me, is what I wanted to shout.
Instead, I said, "Oh yeah, I think it's just a little too early for
me to be rooting around in there."

"For a second, I thought you were going to burst into liquid laughter," Colin said.

"What?"

"You know—technicolour yawn, praying to the porcelain
god, chewing in reverse, or..." Colin paused for a second.
"Rowing and blowing."

He'd obviously just made the last one up; he looked
extremely pleased with himself. I wanted to smack him for
his lack of sympathy. *Better yet, "row and blow" all over him,* I
thought to myself with a chuckle.

I knew the best way to deal with seasickness was to focus on distant objects or the horizon, but foolishly, I spent the next thirty minutes with my head lolling out the hatch and my eyes closed, willing the nausea to pass.

When Colin's two-hour shift at the oars came to an end, I extracted myself from the cabin and slid into the now-empty rowing seat. My feet slipped far too easily into the men's size 10 rowing shoes affixed to the foot plates. The shoes were oversized for me, but they fit Colin well. I grabbed the oars. Once settled, I looked at the cabin-mounted compass and noticed we were no longer pointed in the right direction. The forty-five-second interlude in which we had switched places had been enough to push us off course.

The swell, the wind, and the waves now bullied our heavy boat, and I struggled to correct our position and maintain course. The boat was constantly trying to broach, or turn sideways to the waves, and it seemed I was putting far too much energy into corrective strokes and not enough into direct propulsion. I looked at the GPS, and my heart sank. The 4.5 knots I had achieved in calm waters with a favourable current had dropped to 2. And I was working twice as hard.

The waves were now bigger than they'd been when I was inside the cabin. I wasn't sure if the conditions had changed, or if the waves just appeared larger from this exposed perspective. They crashed against the hull, dousing me with foaming white water. Just as intimidating were the large swells that lifted us to the height of a mid-sized house. These rolling mountains had a wavelength—the distance from the crest of one wave to the next—of several hundred metres, and a height of six metres from trough to peak. Despite the size of these swells, however, they did not rock the boat. Like giant elevators, they gradually lifted and lowered us. It was the turbulence of the smaller waves that rocked us.

"There must be a big storm in the distance creating these swells," Colin guessed.

But forecasters had made no mention of an approaching storm. I hoped they were right. The weather forecast when we departed had been for stable weather, with stiff but manageable winds from the northeast.

Timing is everything when planning an ocean crossing, and we had carefully chosen our window of opportunity. Leave too early and you encounter hurricanes farther south; too late, and it's foul weather off Europe. Hurricanes form in the western regions of the Atlantic Ocean from June to November, while winter storms roll into Portugal and the European coast starting in late September. Although mid-September is the latest recommended time to safely leave the European coast, it is actually the earliest safe departure date when considering the hurricane belt further west. It would take about two months to reach the perimeter of the hurricane region, and our arrival in these lower latitudes would coincide with the end of the hurricane season. Our window of opportunity for avoiding the worst of both seasons was only about two weeks. We had been fortunate to get away in time and, according to pilot charts and hurricane records, our chances of encountering a major storm would be very low.

Considering that our current conditions were called good weather, I was shocked by the turbulence and size of the waves. The towering waves, crashing foam, and violent motion of the boat were what I would have expected of a storm—not a sunny, breezy day off the coast of Lisbon. It made me realize just how much I had to learn about the sea. Clearly, canoeing trips with friends in Canada had done nothing to prepare me for the reality of rowing in the open ocean.

Feelings of anxiety bubbled to the surface, and an annoying voice nagged, *What have you gotten yourself into?* There was no going back. Even if I changed my mind, we could not row against the currents to return to Lisbon. We were completely committed to this row. I created a mantra out of the truism "the greatest rewards come from the greatest commitments," and tried to push the negative thoughts out of my head. They didn't go away easily, though. I had invested an enormous amount of time and all my finances into this endeavour, but I was not prepared to pay the ultimate price.

I focussed on my rowing technique. The words of my Vancouver rowing coach, Alex Binkley, echoed in my mind: "Keep your back straight; push with your legs; increase your speed towards the end of your stroke; don't clench the paddles." But it was harder rowing here than in the calm waters of Coal Harbour. The choppy conditions made it difficult to pull both oars in unison, and waves repeatedly smashed the oars into my legs. If I was a mediocre rower in calm water, I was a dismal rower in ocean chop. And to say I was a moderate rower in civilization was really being kind.

I gave up on technique. It was all I could do to keep moving. I felt exhausted; my arms ached, my knees hurt, and I couldn't imagine rowing for another minute, let alone another several months. I looked at my watch; I had been rowing for thirty minutes.

I tried to distract myself by watching the fishing boats in the distance. I saw close to a dozen, all of them moderate in size and weathered in appearance. I knew that these were small-scale fishing operations, one or two men (I hadn't seen a fisherwoman yet) who went out six days a week—never on Sunday—and sold their catch fresh each day at the local fish markets. They caught mostly sardines, mackerel, and hake, although local octopus, sea bass, tuna, prawns, squid, and swordfish were also for sale at the markets. Most of Portugal's fishermen work in small boats, catching just enough fish to subsist, but they struggle to make a living amid dwindling fish stocks. Today only the bigger and better-equipped boats, which can travel farther in search of fish and stay longer on the water, can prosper (and even their margins are shrinking).

The Portuguese eat more fish per person than any other nationality except for Icelanders, but their fishing industry is in distress as stocks of cod, hake, and whiting are near collapse. They can now no longer meet their own fish needs, relying on imports of dried cod from Norway, sardines from Russia, and stockfish from Iceland.

Sadly, Portugal is not alone in facing this crisis. When I returned to civilization, I heard news reports that this could be the last century of wild seafood. The story was based on the research of an international team of scientists who published their findings in the November 3, 2006 issue of *Science*. They looked at fish catch reports since 1950 in almost all ocean regions, and found that, if the present trend continues, all fish species will decline 90 per cent from their peak numbers by mid-century. Once a population's numbers drop this low, recovery is very difficult, and the species is considered collapsed. If we don't change our approach to managing the oceans, say the scientists, all the world's fish stocks will collapse by 2048.

That's the bad news. The good news is that it doesn't have to be this way. This is not a prediction set in stone, but a warning of what will happen if our approach to the ocean doesn't change. "We can turn this around," said the lead author of the study, Dalhousie University professor Boris Worm. "But less than 1 per cent of the global ocean is effectively protected right now. We won't see complete recovery [in these protected zones] in one year, but in many cases, species will come back more quickly than anticipated—in three to five to ten years. And where this has been done, we see immediate economic benefits." In other words, the costs of managing the oceans responsibly will be infinitely lower for humankind than the cost of continuing our race to catch every last fish.

As I continued rowing, the small fishing boats disappeared from sight. With this last connection to civilization broken, I felt the magnitude of our isolation even more. I looked at Colin sitting inside the cabin and wondered if he, too, worried how we would handle being in this rowboat for months with only each other for company.

IT WAS HARD to decide what was worse: rowing, or lying in the cabin waiting to row. When I was at the oars, all I could think about was how much my body ached and how I wanted the pain to end. But now that I was in the cabin, the pain shifted to other areas. I felt like a teenager who had just discovered the downfall of drinking lemon gin like it was lemonade. I clutched my stomach and closed my eyes, willing myself to ignore the nausea.

Not only was *Ondine* a small boat in big seas, but she lacked many of the stabilizing features of other seagoing vessels. Sailboats, for example, are steadied below the water by a large keel that resists lateral movement, and above the water by the pressure of the wind on the sails. Fishing boats and cruise ships usually have stabilizing fins to counter their natural rolling movement. Our boat, however, had only a tiny keel and no sails. The smallest wave sent it rocking and pitching.

As I lay in the cabin, waiting for my rowing shift to begin, I examined the foam-padded ceiling and read the pen scribbles barely an arm's length above me. The previous owners had left phone numbers, short checklists, and, right in the middle, a jailhouse calendar composed of fifty-six dashes—one for each day of *Ondine's* previous voyage from the Canaries to the Caribbean islands. Our journey, from mainland to mainland, would be double the distance and would likely take twice as long. It still seemed incomprehensible that we were spending a single night in this rowboat, let alone any number of months. I prematurely started our own countdown and marked off day one with a permanent marker. Then I nodded off, escaping to a dream world that didn't include rowboats and waves.

"Five minutes!" Colin yelled.

The world came spinning and rocking back into focus. I slipped my cycling gloves onto my already-blistered hands.

"How are things coming along out there?" I asked.

"Lots of shipping," Colin replied. "We've had several freighters pass quite close to us. You can still see land, but it's getting low."

"How about Miami?"

"What about Miami?"

"Can you see it yet?"

"Almost. I think it's just over the horizon." Colin looked over his left shoulder, brow furrowed. It almost looked like he really was searching for the sandy shores of Florida.

"Ex-lax!" he suddenly exclaimed.

"Huh?"

"Ex-lax," Colin repeated. "We forgot to get *laxatives!*"

"Oops!" I said.

I remembered all too clearly our bid to purchase laxatives. The clerk in the pharmacy spoke no English (which is rare in Portugal). He didn't understand what we were asking for, and finally Colin was forced to mime what the product was used for. It was funny and embarrassing at the same time. Unfortunately the pharmacy had none in stock, and we had to try elsewhere. But we forgot.

Our diet would be devoid of fresh fruits and vegetables, and very high in low-fibre carbohydrates. I shuddered at the thought of having problems thousands of kilometres away from any medical facilities or pharmacies.

"I remember reading the book *Lost* by Thomas Thompson," Colin said. "Their trimaran flipped and they were living in the overturned hull. The woman was suffering from extreme constipation, and it reached the point where her husband had to reach in and remove a stool the size of a baseball."

This conversation wasn't helping me reach peace with our new lifestyle.

"How the hell do you just *reach in* and grab a turd the size of softball?" I snapped.

"*Baseball*," Colin corrected. "I don't know—that's just what it said."

I made a mental note of where we stored the prunes and slid out the hatch to begin my shift. Miami seemed a long way away.

BACK AT THE oars, I felt uncoordinated and exhausted. The waves seemed to be even larger from this vantage point, and far too often an oar would get caught on a wave and slam into my leg. Normally, both oars would be balanced when I pulled them through the water during my stroke, but now I found it easier to put one slightly ahead of the other. This allowed me to get the oars a little higher out of the water, and prevented unnecessary damage to my thighs. I was sure this was a big no-no in terms of rowing technique and would dash my dreams of arriving home a rowing champion. My dreams were quickly fading.

From my outside vantage, I looked directly at the cabin. Colin's long, sun-bleached hair poked out the partially open Plexiglas hatch as he lay on his side, munching on crackers. Although his hair was blond, his beard was mostly red, and now that it was thick and bushy, he looked like a savage Viking. And, indeed, the blood of the Norse warriors possibly did flow through his veins. His mother and father are both Scottish—their families came from Caithness, an area once settled by Scandinavians.

I couldn't help but wonder if a seafaring heritage makes a difference to one's level of comfort on the ocean. Colin's father was a sea captain, and many of his relatives worked in the fishing industry. I, however, come from a family devoid of any Captain High Liners. My mother comes from a farming region in a landlocked part of Germany, my father from a large city in Syria, and, as far I knew, the closest anyone in their families got to a water-based job was when the farm fields were irrigated.

Even if nature took a back seat to nurture, I was no further ahead. Although Colin did not meet his seafaring father until he was an adult, his mother is equally adventurous, and she instilled him with a love of the outdoors through hikes in the mountains and along Vancouver Island's coast. Even today, in her seventies, she is a very active member of the Comox chapter of the B.C. Mountaineering Club. She consistently places near the top of her age group in running races. In comparison, my family was both sedentary and interior. My father equated the outdoors with discomfort; he had spent too much time in military arctic survival courses. My mother worried that outdoor activity was unhealthy and would make me sick, or that some other unforeseen danger would befall me. Now they both shake their heads and wonder where in the child-raising process they erred.

A LARGE WAVE crashed over the boat, wrenching me off the rowing seat and away from my thoughts. I grabbed the life-lines for balance and struggled back onto the rowing seat. I glanced quickly at the navigational equipment to ensure we were still on the correct course.

We relied on a brand new chartplotter/GPS (Global Positioning System) that we'd affixed outside, alongside the compass. The GPS was undoubtedly the most important navigational tool we had, indicating our coordinates, speed, and direction using satellite technology. Because of the one- or two-second delay in the GPS output, it was easier to keep the boat on course by looking at the magnetic compass, which reacted instantly as the boat moved.

"What do you want for dinner?" Colin asked, propping the hatch door open so he could access the single-burner alcohol stove that sat between the cabin hatch and the sliding seat.

I questioned the feasibility of cooking in these rough conditions, but Colin seemed optimistic, and he was the one with the extensive seafaring experience.

"We're going to be eating pretty limited fare until it gets a little calmer," he said. "Most of our food is stored under the deck hatches, and there's no way we're going to get to it until things calm down."

I surveyed the constant flow of water sluicing over the decks, ebbing and flowing as the waves passed by. Our boat felt unnervingly like a submarine sitting at the surface: barely buoyant, and ready to go down at any time.

"I didn't realize having this much weight in our boat would be such a problem," I said.

"We'll be eating forty pounds of food a week. We'll be sitting higher out of the water in no time."

Colin decided on a menu of stew and rice. The rice simmered in a pot of water. Just before the grains were fully tender, he added a can of stew, which would be hot by the time the rice was completely cooked. The appealing scent of garlic and gravy wafted across the boat. Then, just as I was savouring the prospect of our first hot meal of the voyage, a sinister snarl announced a larger-than-average wave bearing down on us. It hit the side of the boat with a surly *thwack*, and buckets of salty water cascaded over me and the open cooking pot.

With delusional optimism, Colin stuck his spoon into the stew-turned-soup and brought it to his lips. His face scrunched up in disgust and he spit the contents of his mouth over the side. Sputtering more words of disdain, he tossed the stew overboard, and we postponed our hot meal to another day.

The ocean's mineral concentration includes 3.5 per cent salt, which offends more than our taste buds. In large quantities, salt becomes a toxin; twelve grams is enough to kill a human being. The daily recommended limit is five hundred milligrams, which means a single teaspoon of seawater contains enough salt for the whole day.

Salt toxicity is not a problem in civilization, where even the most ardent enthusiast of pretzels and bar nuts could not come close to consuming a lethal amount. On the ocean, however, sodium chloride has claimed countless souls. Lost sailors on a desert of brine often give in to temptation and greedily gulp at the sea beneath them. These fleeting moments of pleasure—filling their bellies with cool water—are soon replaced with their final wretched moments of agony and despair. When salt enters the body, it is absorbed quickly into the bloodstream. If there's too much sodium chloride, our cells and organs give up their water to dilute it, becoming dehydrated and eventually dying. Meanwhile, the kidneys try to filter out the salt, but they shut down when the accumulated salt levels are too high. Finally, the salt-poisoned become delusional as their brains swell, and they are racked with seizures until death from kidney failure or multiple organ collapse.

Instead of salty stew, we dined on peanut butter sandwiches made with heavily processed white bread. The expiration date for the bread was still three weeks away, and it contained enough preservatives to sink a small rowboat.

"If we eat any more of this bread, we're going to have multiple organ failure anyway," I said. But unless the weather improved, we would not be cooking anything; really, we were lucky to have brought such a large supply of bread to see us through.

SHORTLY BEFORE 9:00 PM, darkness enveloped the boat. Colin was rowing, and I peered outside through the hatch door, grateful to be inside and wrapped in a blanket. The overcast sky shed little light, and the moon had not yet risen. I could still see the surface of the water, but barely.

"Can you turn the boat lights on?" Colin asked. I flipped the switch for the compass light, and a faint glow illuminated the dial. The button for the strobe light was in our electrical panel, and I searched before locating the right one. Bright, pulsating light washed over the boat and into the darkness. It would be hard for other boats not to spot us; I just hoped they wouldn't misinterpret our flashing light for a distress signal.

"How is it out there?" I asked.

"The waves are building, but we're making good speed. We're doing between 2.8 and 3 knots."

"I'll plot our position if you can tell me what our coordinates are," I said.

I turned on the cabin light and unclipped the rolled-up chart from its hold on the ceiling. We had several charts with us, including those of Portugal, Lisbon Harbour, the Canary Islands, and Miami Harbour. I unrolled a large-scale depiction of Portugal's coastal waters. The chart took up most of the room in the cabin, so I balanced awkwardly above it and used the straight edge of a book to find the intersection point of our latitude and longitude coordinates. I marked it with a tiny X.

"Our direction is perfect. We've travelled forty-six kilometres southwest of Lisbon," I announced.

"That's great. Let's hope these winds keep coming from this direction."

We were angling our boat so that we could get away from the Portuguese coastline as quickly as possible. As long as we were near land, we were in danger. Since we had no motor or sails, we relied on the relatively feeble power of our oars. The winds could switch at any time and, if sufficiently strong, they could push us into the rocky coast to be shipwrecked. Sustained strong winds from the west, northwest, or southwest within the next two days would spell trouble.

By the time it was my shift again, the darkness was complete, broken only by the glow of Lisbon in the distance and the navigation lights of several far-away freighters. These ghostly reminders of civilization served only to make me feel more alone in the inky blackness. The roar of waves filled my ears, but I could no longer see the features of the water. In the darkness the ocean felt wilder, and cold tendrils of fear enveloped me. I would not spend my first night ensconced in a warm secure bed; instead, I would bump along in a wave-tossed rowboat, thousands of kilometres from land.

I wondered why humans seem to have a primal fear of the dark. Was it an evolutionary adaptation to help keep us from harm's way while sabre-toothed tigers and other nocturnal predators hunted? Even though we no longer need to worry about prowling cats, there's no denying that things get a little creepier at night—whether on a walk alone in the woods or during a night house-sitting in a lonely farmhouse. Darkness makes you feel alone, vulnerable, impotent. Unidentifiable sounds tease the imagination and set the heart racing. On land, darkness is bearable. But on the ocean, where the very act of being suspended by liquid thousands of metres above the sea floor feels unnatural, the mind truly struggles with the absence of light.

I listened to the waves, trying to decide which one would be big enough to soak me. *Phoooshhh.* It was loud, and I cringed with anticipation. Nothing. Another *whoooshhh.* Then an odd, sudden silence preceded a thunderous crack, and churning water foamed over the boat. Cold water soaked my hair and dribbled down my shirt. I shivered in the cool night air and picked up my speed to warm up. I knew the waning gibbous moon would be rising now, but its radiance was obscured behind a thick curtain of clouds. I stared out at the waves, trying in vain to discern their size. Then, out of the corner of my eye, I thought I saw something in the water, but I couldn't be sure. It looked large and had a different motion from the waves. *Was it a shark?* I knew the chances of a shark attacking a person—let alone a boat—were minuscule, but suddenly, in the darkness, it seemed all too likely. *What would I do if a shark attacked the boat?* I tried to calm myself thinking about statistics I had read earlier.

According to the International Shark Attack File, between fifty and eighty shark attacks occur annually around the world, resulting in an average of five deaths per year since 1990. In other words, only one person out of a billion dies from a shark attack annually. You are at a higher risk of being killed by lightning, bee stings, dogs, toasters, and farmyard pigs. Of course, one might argue that you can't compare terrestrial and marine injury statistics. R. Aidan Martin from the ReefQuest

Centre for Shark Research found that even in the water, shark attack is among the least likely of perils—140,000 people die from drowning each year, and surfers are more likely to injure themselves on their boards than to be injured by a shark. Yet in the darkness I found little reassurance in risk assessment statistics. Instead, my mind replayed scenes from the horror movie *Jaws* as vividly as an IMAX screen.

Ironically, from a logical standpoint, sharks have more reason to fear us than we have to fear them. Each year, humans kill 100 million sharks. In a single century, we have had a much more dramatic impact on the shark population than millions of years of natural challenges. Oceanic white-tip sharks that used to be commonly sighted in these waters are now increasingly scarce. The IUCN lists these sharks as vulnerable and reports tremendous declines—99.3 per cent since the 1950s in certain regions. However, the exact number is under debate because changing fishing practices complicate the analysis. Sadly, many species of sharks have suffered a similar fate. All species of large coastal sharks—nurse, bull, lemon, blacktip, sandbar, hammerhead, and great white—have declined between 50 and 90 per cent since the 1970s, according to a study that appeared in the March 30, 2007 edition of the journal *Science*.

The impact of losing this great predator of the sea should be more frightening than the remote possibility of actually encountering a hungry shark. Large sharks are at the top of the ocean food chain, which means they play a key role in regulating the populations of other species. But their numbers are now too low to fulfill that obligation. As a result, populations of creatures they feed on—rays, skates, smaller sharks, and others—have exploded.

Nothing leapt out of the water at me, and I tried to subdue my hyperactive imagination by focussing on rowing. I maintained my course by keeping Lisbon's glow at a forty-five-degree angle to my stern, and occasionally squinted to calibrate the compass heading. Tomorrow, we would be too far from shore to see those lights. Instead, we would be surrounded by a horizon of uninterrupted black. For navigation, we would rely completely on our compass or GPS. I practised using our GPS now, but found it much more difficult than using a distant reference point. It was a little like driving blindfolded while your passenger relays instructions.

It took all my energy to keep rowing until the end of my shift. I couldn't remember ever anticipating bedtime with such enthusiasm. I woke Colin, slipped into the warm spot he vacated, and passed out. Two hours later, at 2:00 AM, Colin joined me in the cabin. He had lashed the oars to the deck and tightened the rudder. We would free-drift for a few hours while we both caught some shut-eye. Since we were moving with the prevailing winds and currents, we hoped we wouldn't lose too much ground. We still wouldn't sleep soundly, as we would have to take watches for ships every half-hour. Colin would be on watch duty tonight. He set the stopwatch to thirty minutes. I closed the ceiling hatch and locked the main hatch in the vent position. The vent position gave us just enough air circulation to breathe and, if a big wave hit, it would prevent the cabin from being flooded. We had already turned on our bright strobe light, which would keep other boats at a safe distance as long as no one was tempted to investigate.

"Congratulations on your first day—you're doing amazing," Colin said as he struggled out of his damp shirt.

"You, too, babe."

I lay my head on Colin's chest, wrapped my arm around him, and murmured, "I love you." It felt strange and familiar at the same time: just another night sleeping in our usual positions. I was surprised at how safe and comfortable I suddenly felt. The boat rocked at a rate somewhere between cradle and carnival ride, but we were held in position by the encroaching gear and barely moved. Colin's heart beat reassuringly against my ear; his breathing deepened with sleep's arrival, and I soon joined him.

5

A NEAR MISS
IN BUSY WATERS

FUMBLED FOR THE off button on my beeping wristwatch
alarm, relieved at the return to silence. Just as if I were
on holiday, waking up in a strange bed, I felt momentarily puzzled: *Where am I?* It didn't take long to realize that
I wasn't dreaming anymore, that I was finally on the ocean.
My grogginess vanished in a heartbeat, replaced with enormous satisfaction. Now, instead of tedious preparation and
worrying that we'd never leave in time, I looked forward to
an incredible adventure.

But my euphoria was short-lived. I soon realized I was
to take first shift on the oars. It was 6:00 AM and still dark.
The waves outside rumbled threateningly. I yearned to pull
the blankets over my head and sleep for another hour. I
enviously eyed Colin's sleeping form as I rummaged for my
windbreaker, pants, baseball cap, and cycling gloves. I ate
a handful of crackers before reluctantly crawling out of the
cabin. A shrill wind whipped through the cables while the

waves slurped and gurgled like a hungry monster. I gripped the safety line as I moved about the deck to unfasten the oars. The open-cell foam rubber padding on the rowing seat had absorbed water like a sponge. As it compressed under my weight, water squirted out, soaking my pants. The shoes, too, were wet and cold, and I cringed as I slid my bare, blistered feet into them. There was no point in wearing socks, as they would be soaked in minutes. I leaned back, gripped the oar handles, and slid them outboard until the collar hit the oarlock with a satisfying *thunk*.

I wrestled with the oars, slowly pointed the bow southeast, and fell into the rhythm of the row. Exertion pumped heat into my body and cleared the dread that had set in with the night. My monochrome world gradually transformed, and a pink glow hinted at the coming sun. I watched, mesmerized, as the sun slowly rose, alighting the clouds and casting a lone beam of light across the sea.

Colin slept soundly in the cabin, wrapped up in the blankets, with the hatch firmly shut. His long blond hair poked out from beneath the blankets, but that was the only part of him I could see. I loved watching Colin sleep. Even though I couldn't see his face, I imagined his relaxed face, his partially open mouth and deep breaths, his chest gently rising and lowering. I don't know why, but it made me think about how much I loved him.

Before leaving, I had been filled with worry about what this journey would do to our relationship. Some of my friends' relationships have disintegrated on vacation. When I told my father my plans, he said, "Don't do it. You will never get married if you go on this expedition together. Stay home and wait for him."

Colin and I first met three years before, when we both lived in Vancouver. On a drizzly Friday night in September, I was bored and half-heartedly perused the guide from our local second-run cinema. The show that night read, "Special Event. Raft the Amazon with Colin Angus—tickets $10 (advance)/$12 (door). Show: 8:00 PM." I looked at my watch; it was 7:40 PM. I had never heard of Colin Angus, but it sounded more fun than sitting at home.

I arrived just as the show was beginning and took a spot near the front of the Ridge Theatre's seven hundred seats. The theatre was full and my prime real estate was courtesy of being a party of one. The lights dimmed and a young guy stepped on stage. *He must be the introducer,* I thought.

"Thank you for coming out tonight. My name is Colin Angus..."

I was surprised. He seemed too young... and too small. When I thought of adventurers, I pictured Grizzly Adams or maybe Indiana Jones. At least he (or she) had to have wrinkles and look capable of fighting off a grizzly bear, bare-handed at that.

As Colin's tale unfolded, I became entranced, and not only by his descriptions of the Amazon Basin. When Colin was eleven years old, he decided to sail around the world. He was inspired by a library book—*Dove*—written by a young man, Robin Lee Graham, who did just that as a teenager. But Colin lived in a blue-collar mill town in British Columbia, with a single working mom who was raising four kids; there was little to drive his dream except his own will. At fifteen he bought a small sailboat with his paper-route earnings, and four years later he bought a slightly larger boat with his tree-planting money. When he left Vancouver Island in his decrepit boat, almost everyone thought he was foolish, stupid, or both. People told him he would die, and when that didn't dissuade him, they told his mother he was suicidal. The mantra "100 per cent demise, guaranteed" played in the minds of his farewell party. Colin spent five years sailing, meandering south along America's west coast to Mexico, across the Pacific Ocean, around Australia, and amid tropical islands.

When he returned to Canada, Colin—unable to stay away from the library—became seduced by tales of the Amazon River, and decided to raft it from beginning to end. Lacking the ability to whitewater raft did not cross his mind as a serious hurdle, nor did gun-toting rebels, class-five whitewater, or a financially challenged bank account. He found facts in books, saved his pennies, and learned to raft while becoming a guide on the Kananaskis River near Canmore, Alberta. Only one previous team had successfully navigated the full Amazon, although many had tried and failed with fatal consequences. And all these expeditions were well financed, equipped with cutting-edge equipment, and teamed with experienced athletes.

Again, despite popular advice to the contrary, Colin and two friends left with a whitewater raft, a video camera his sister had given them, and almost no money. Colin read the camera manual on the plane, and in Peru he hit the record button for the first time. Five months later they reached the Atlantic Ocean and he returned home. The documentary I watched came from that footage and was edited on his home computer with trial software. Somehow he had also managed to write a book during the time he wasn't working his day job, editing the film, or planning his next adventure. Three years had passed since his Amazon voyage, and since then, he'd been on a few more hair-raising adventures, made another film, and written his second book.

Why can't I ever meet guys like this? I mused. But it was more than Colin's love of the outdoors or his willingness to explore its remotest corners that captivated me; it was his compulsion to do things that at first glance seemed impossible. And I loved that he didn't take on these challenges rashly. Instead, he diligently researched them and acquired the needed skills before reaching the conclusion that *Yes, this is possible.* Then, despite setbacks, limited finances, and opposing public opinion, he stuck to his plan and never gave up.

I walked out of the theatre, passing the table of his books in the foyer, and thought, *Hmmm, I guess I should support his next journey.* I bought *Amazon Extreme* for twenty dollars and went back into the theatre to get it signed. A group of people circled Colin, asking questions about his journey. I hovered at the perimeter, waiting my turn. He turned to glance at me while listening to a question. He did the same thing during the next question. My ears started to feel hot, and I had the sinking suspicion I was blushing. There was a slight pause in the questioning, and he turned to me.

I racked my brain for all the questions I had, but, afflicted with acute amnesia, I resorted to probably the most frequently asked question: "So, ahhh, ummm, what was your favourite part of the trip?" He graciously answered my lame query as if it was the first time he'd heard such a brilliant inquiry. Finally my neurons haphazardly started to fire, and I remembered the things I was curious about. "How long did you have to stay with the armed men who captured you in

Peru? How did you get your stolen video camera back? What is your upcoming expedition?" Shyness prevented me from asking the question I really wanted to ask.

"Who should I make this out to?" Colin asked, reaching for my book.

"Julie."

"Do you have any trips planned?"

My mind blanked, and I panicked. I was supposed to climb Mount Rainier during my holidays the following week, but that had been cancelled. *What were those ski trips I wanted to do this winter? Does going home to visit my parents at Christmas count?* "Turkey, I'm going to Turkey next year," I blurted, relieved that comprehensible words had exited my mouth.

I'd been to Istanbul once and had long dreamed of returning, but that was as far into planning as I had ventured.

"Well, I hope you have a good time," Colin said, handing the book back to me.

"Good luck on your next expedition."

There was an awkward pause, almost like neither of us wanted this chance encounter to be our only time together. Well, I could say with certainty that one of us felt that way; less than a year later, I found out it was mutual.

The next time I saw Colin was on a drizzly spring morning in Vancouver. I was standing at the bus stop, wearing shorts and a T-shirt. Two other Lycra-clad people waited at the street corner with me. We all had numbers pinned to our chests, indicating a shared destiny for the next three hours. The fourth person to join our group walked up with one of the most extreme duck-footed strides I'd ever seen. He was fit, but based on his footwear, which looked more like five-dollar Kmart sneaker cast-offs than proper running shoes, I wrongly deduced that he wasn't running the ten-kilometre Vancouver Sun Run. And with a walk like that, who could blame him?

We all waited quietly. Occasionally one of us would excitedly blurt, "There's a bus—maybe we'll get on this one." That was swiftly followed by, "This one's full too."

Bus after bus passed, packed full of runners, while the drivers shook their heads at us.

Then Duck-foot said, "At this rate, I don't think we'll make it in time for the start of the race. Maybe we should start walking and then try to catch a bus on Burrard Street, where it might be less crowded." So he *was* doing the run.

"Great idea," I said.

As we walked, chatter flowed, and I overheard Duck-foot say, "I haven't been running much lately, because I've been on the road doing film presentations."

The bulb went off in my head. "I saw you talk at the Ridge Theatre last year! Your show about the Amazon was great."

He looked at me, eyes focussed. "Hey, that's right. You were going to Turkey."

I was thrilled. I couldn't believe he remembered me. He must have met thousands of people on his tour and hundreds that night alone.

"I actually never went to Turkey, but I'm going to Nepal next week," I said.

"That'll be amazing. I've always been interested in Nepal."

"I'll be hiking to Everest Base Camp, and then travelling in the Annapurna mountain range. I'll be travelling solo," I added, trying to hint at my single status without sounding like I had no friends.

I was about to put my foot in my mouth when Colin mercifully interjected.

"Maybe you can show me your photos when you get back?"

"That would be great."

I felt like a kid on Christmas morning. The next day I told a friend at work, "I've met the guy I'm going to marry." I've never really believed in love at first sight, and I've always been rather bad at gauging people from initial impressions, but this time was different. It seemed like uncanny good fortune, or what some might call fate, had brought us together. We wooed each other with canoe trips in Indian Arm, hikes in the nearby mountain ranges, and runs along Kitsilano Beach. Ten months later we were engaged, and two and a half years later, I found myself on the Atlantic Ocean with my beloved duck-footed runner.

BEFORE I KNEW it, the sun was fully above the horizon, and my two-hour rowing shift was over.

"Good morning, Colin," I said in a loud, happy voice.

"Your congenial greeting is a very, very thin veil for what you really wish to communicate," Colin quickly retorted without a hint of grogginess as he peered between greasy smudges on the hatch. "How are things out there?"

"The winds are the same as yesterday, about force three, and they're still coming from the north-northeast. Our speed is great, 2.5 knots. But it's not easy rowing; it's choppy, and the boat keeps pulling to the portside."

"Have you tried adjusting the rudder?"

"Yeah, but it didn't help," I grumbled. "We need an autopilot."

"Or how about a big outboard?"

"Maybe an outboard and a bigger boat," I said.

"Damn," Colin laughed, "we should have got a big power

boat with a bunch of servants on board. That'd be the way to cross the Atlantic in comfort."

"God help us," I said, glancing over our submersible-cum-rowboat. "Why *did* we do this to ourselves? We've put a man on the moon, and yet we two morons decide to step back a few millennia in technology and row across an ocean."

I was feeling good now. Somehow, making fun of our enterprise was delightfully satisfying, especially with the prospect of my shift about to end.

"Yeah, but those astronauts could barely walk when they got back from the moon. Just think how much exercise you're getting. In three or four months when we get to the other side, you'll be looking like the Governator."

Three or four months! I still had trouble comprehending this reality and would have been really disturbed if I knew the journey would take even longer. I tried not to think about it, and instead pondered what I would make for breakfast.

Unfortunately I was feeling just as nauseous as the day before, and my appetite was weak. Seasickness is an insidious condition brought about by contradictory sensory stimuli. Normally the information from our eyes and inner ears that we use to maintain our balance matches, but in a boat, all that arithmetic goes out the window. The boat appears to be still, so our eyes tell us we're stationary, while the receptors in our ears report vigorous motion. The brain has trouble interpreting this conflicting information, and the result is a feeling of extreme nausea, lethargy, and sickness—like a bad hangover without the fun of the night before.

I'd spent the previous day hoping that mental fortitude could conquer seasickness. Now I relinquished that misguided theory and took a double dose of dimenhydrinate (more commonly known as Gravol). This drug suppresses feelings of nausea and sickness by blocking histamine levels. For good measure, I added a painkiller to quell my caffeine-withdrawal headache.

Colin, too, opted for treatment and applied a medicated patch behind his ear, where it would release a continuous stream of scopolamine for three days. Scopolamine is a drug derived from plants in the nightshade family; it works by interfering with certain nerve receptors in the ear. How it works is not fully understood, but the theory is that the slight interference in balance receptors helps the brain to better cope with the conflicting signals.

After half an hour, I felt marginally better. I was still far from completely recovered, but the rest of the day progressed with less discomfort. The day blurred by in a medley of rowing, eating, and sleeping. Our last ties to land and civilization quickly faded. I could no longer see the coastline of Portugal or the lights of Lisbon. We saw no fishing boats, only the occasional outline of a larger boat far in the distance. Nature was gradually replacing the creations of humankind. We watched birds soar on air currents, and in the sea we saw infrequent glimmers of silver—the majestic tuna.

It was exciting to see the tuna jump, and the first few times I yelled for Colin to come on deck to watch. A few different kinds of tuna live in these waters, including bluefin, bigeye, albacore, and skipjack, and it is possible to distinguish between the different types by their coloration, size, and length of dorsal fin. But I wasn't able to, and since Colin had spent time working on a B.C. fishboat, I hoped he would have more success than me. Unfortunately, the fish were too far away, and he could only guess. Given that we were still in subtropical waters not far from the Mediterranean, we hypothesized that some of the tuna might be Atlantic bluefin, which spawn in the Mediterranean and then migrate across the Atlantic. These fish can travel up to seventy kilometres per hour and cross the Atlantic Ocean in less than sixty days. I was rather envious of their speed.

It is hard not to be enamoured of these lightning-fast creatures, by their beauty and grace—and by their taste. This last attribute causes the bluefin tuna much trouble. The size, colour, texture, and high fat content of the so-called "king of fish" make them highly prized, especially for sushi.

Bluefin tuna are harvested in great numbers, both legally and illegally. Modern fishing practices are extraordinarily efficient and, according to California's Monterey Bay Aquarium, have caused the world bluefin population to plunge 90 per cent since 1970. Scientists and conservationists are working hard to reverse this trend, by encouraging the lowering of fishing quotas, cessation of illegal fishing, and protection of breeding grounds. But so far, not one unified organization or government has implemented the required changes.

The International Commission for the Conservation of Atlantic Tunas (ICCAT) is responsible for the management of tuna, but according to the World Wide Fund for Nature (WWF), they don't do a good job of it. The WWF criticizes the ICCAT for setting irresponsibly high quotas—in 2007 they were twice as high as scientifically recommended—and for continuing to allow fishing during peak spawning season. That's not to say firmer regulations would help much; many nations flaunt the laws, and, with no one to adequately monitor and enforce regulations, illegal fishing is rampant. Many believe bluefin tuna fishery in the East Atlantic and

Mediterranean is out of control, that the most basic requirements for fisheries management are absent, and that the
industry is in fact unregulated.

"It is the most scandalous case of fisheries mismanagement
currently happening in the world," said Dr. Sergi Tudela of
the WWF in 2007. The industry was rife with fishing during
the closed season, illegal use of spotter planes, massive overfishing, and an international ring of corruption to conceal
illegal catches.

The small school of jumping tuna had long disappeared
from our sight. I hoped they would lead long lives. They
were off in chase of flying fish, herring, and sardines, flit-
ting beneath the water at speeds we could only dream of. I
wondered if they swam nearby or were already miles away. It
was impossible to see more than a few metres into the water
directly next to us. What lay beneath the water seemed such
a mystery.

THE FORCE OF the wind grew. It created intimidating waves
that rammed the oar handles into my bruised shins. The
waves toppled onto the boat, striking me with their foaming
plumes. I was suddenly scared of the sea, of how quickly it had
grown. The darkness of our third night out settled in, and I
felt no more comfortable now than I had the two nights before.
On the contrary, the sea seemed even more wicked tonight.

Colin agreed, and we lashed the oars to the boat at midnight, two hours earlier than we would normally have. We
huddled in the cabin—Colin on his back, me on my side—
trying to get comfortable in our unbearably cramped quarters. Sleep did not come easily, so I listened to the powerful
wind and waves.

In the morning I climbed out of the cabin and into the gusting winds. Waves sprayed me as I unfastened the oars and settled into the rowing seat. But I struggled to keep the boat on course. I cursed the rudder. If only I could control it while rowing, keeping the boat on course would not be such an issue. But I had only the oars to pivot an eight-hundred-kilogram boat against forty-kilometre-an-hour winds and two-metre waves. After almost an hour of futile and exhausting rowing, I gave up. It was time to deploy the sea anchor.

In rough, stormy conditions it is best to point the bow of the boat into the wind and waves using a sea anchor or drogue. A drogue is essentially an underwater parachute connected to the bow with a long shock-absorbing line. As the wind pushes the boat, the boat naturally weathercocks towards the drogue. A regular anchor would also cause the boat to swing into the wind and waves, but of course, using a conventional anchor isn't feasible in the middle of the ocean's depths.

I struggled to the front of the boat through driving rain and spray and opened the forward compartment where the drogue was stored. Our boat was currently broaching (sitting sideways to the waves) and in a very vulnerable position. Waves crashed over the boat, rocking it violently. I tied the loose end of the rope to an eye ring on the bow and then slipped the conical canvas drogue into the water. The ghostly shape slipped into the distance until it reached the end of the line. Suddenly there was tension on the line, and the boat began nosing into the waves. The result was a little disappointing. We had hoped that, with the drogue, the boat would be perpendicular to the waves. Instead, it sat at about a sixty-degree angle to the ideal angle of attack.

I climbed back into the cabin, absolutely drenched, and huddled against Colin's warmth as the whistling wind increased in intensity. We ate our breakfast of salted soda crackers, cheese, and cured ham. Neither of us felt like doing any of our daily chores (plotting our position on the charts, writing in our journals, making water with the desalinator). Instead we lay sandwiched together in the cabin, bumping into each other and the walls as waves collided with our boat.

"I have to go pee," I informed Colin glumly.

"Yeah, I have to offload some cargo myself, but I think I'll..."

Colin was interrupted by the thunderous explosion of an enormous breaking wave. Our vessel rolled almost ninety degrees, and I was thrown on top of Colin. Books, charts, boxes of crackers, and waterproof electronic cases toppled onto us. Slowly the boat righted, and I could see the water gushing off the decks through the scuppers.

"Holy shit, that was a big one," I said.

The pressure in my bladder was greater than ever, and I feared another giant wave might trigger the inevitable. There was no way I could pee in a bucket in the cabin. (I had trouble peeing in those little jars doctors issued, and that was in the privacy of an immobile bathroom.) Even when the weather was calm, I'd had trouble dealing with my toilet needs on this trip. Initially, I'd imagined we would use a bucket on the deck. (Colin always talked about the "bucket and chuck it" days back in his sailboat. He forgot to mention the importance of partially filling the bucket with water in advance, and my first attempt had been very messy indeed.)

I soon learned that the best way to go to the bathroom on a rowboat was to hang my derriere over the side while sitting on the outer rail. The lifelines made a secure backrest, and it was much more relaxing than using the bucket. Now, however, in gale-force winds, just being outside was a precarious experience.

"I'm going out. I can't hold my bladder any longer," I informed Colin.

"Just make sure you tie yourself on," Colin said, looking worried.

I nodded. We had a thick six-metre length of rope with one end secured to the boat for conditions like this. I tied the free end around my waist with a secure bowline knot. If I was washed off the decks, this would be my umbilical cord to safety. I waited for a lull between waves and quickly dashed out of the cabin, shutting the hatch securely behind me. I sat on the outer rail and relaxed my bladder—relief. Momentarily incapacitated by nature's call, I watched in disbelief as a perfectly formed cresting wave reared towards me. I tightened my grip on the safety line. The wave poured over me and the boat rolled portside from the impact, dipping me up to my waist in the ocean. I clung to the lifeline while the boat slowly righted, and then I pulled up my dripping spandex shorts and scurried back into the cabin.

"All is well?" Colin asked.

"Better than well." I was feeling invigorated. "I've learned that our classy bathroom is not only self-flushing, but it also comes with a powerful bidet."

BY MID-AFTERNOON THE weather had not changed. While Colin rummaged for food, I decided to make some space for him by going outside to check the drogue. I tugged on the line, surprised at how little tension there was. Concerned,

I began pulling in the remaining eighty metres of rope. I hoped for a logical explanation that would include a sea anchor at the rope's terminus. Perhaps the lines had tangled and the anchor collapsed.

But it wasn't long before my suspicions were confirmed. Our anchor was gone. In its place were a few tatters of red cloth clinging to a swivel. The very weather it was supposed to protect us from had destroyed it—alarmingly, it was only our fourth day out.

Colin retrieved our sole backup drogue, affixed it to the swivel, and dropped it overboard. We inspected the replacement several times throughout the day and it seemed to fare better than its predecessor. By the following morning, its services were no longer needed.

ON THE SIXTH day the winds picked up again, and our exercise was limited to rolling around the cabin. Adding insult to injury, my period started. I was sore, my back ached, and my muscles felt stiff, as though I'd been sitting in an economy plane seat for several around-the-world flights. I was irritable. Colin was grumpy. I moaned about aches and pains while Colin, who is amazingly oblivious to physical discomforts, grumbled mostly about our lack of progress. There was tension in the cabin, and we were becoming short with each other. So far on this expedition, we hadn't had any major fights, but this situation put our relationship to the test. We wanted to row, not to be thrashed around like we were in a barrel careening over endless rapids. Originally we planned to row twenty hours a day or more, and now we seemed to be averaging half that. We were worried that this slow pace would extend our trip. If this kept up, we would have to start rationing our food supplies soon.

The winds blew at about forty-five kilometres per hour. They had been between force three and six on the Beaufort scale since we'd left. Force three is a gentle breeze (twelve to nineteen kilometres an hour) with waves of 0.6 metres. This was ideal for rowing. At force four, winds are between twenty and twenty-nine kilometres and waves are about 1 metre. Waves would regularly crash into the boat, making it a little harder to stay on course. At force five, wind speeds increased to thirty to thirty-nine kilometres an hour, and waves doubled in size to over 2 metres. And now we were in force six conditions—wind speeds of forty to fifty kilometres an hour and waves 3 metres high with foam sprays off their crests. Small craft advisories are issued in force six conditions, and rowing is pretty much futile.

By the morning of day seven, we had been cooped up in the cabin for thirty-six hours. Imagine spending a day and a half with your partner, lying in a standard bathtub—which is actually more spacious than our cabin was at the time. At first it's somewhat comfortable, even a relief to just relax. But then you start shifting, trying to find a comfortable position. You lie on your back until an ache in your lower vertebrae forces you to roll onto your side, but soon your hip bone is sore from the pressure. You try to shift the weight more onto your thigh by extending your leg, but then you kick your partner. You both grumble about how small it is. Then you discuss body arrangements that might lead to more comfort, and through a coordinated effort you switch positions so that your head is at the other end of the tub. Your partner's feet are in your face, but you don't care; surprisingly, they smell less than you remember.

Finally, on day eight, the low-pressure system moved on and the violent motion of the boat began to diminish.

"I think it's getting better," I said.

"It seems to be. I'll haul up the sea anchor and try rowing," Colin said.

"Sounds good. I'll make breakfast."

With great effort, I propped open the hatch to reach the stove. Something was wrong. Instead of looking out into a heaving sea, a solid wall of blue lay to my left. For a split second I thought a rogue wave was about to destroy us. Then I realized it wasn't a wave—it was the hull of a freighter. The wall of blue was steel and just metres away, about to crush us. I screamed—a long, loud, piercing scream.

"What's going on?" Colin yelled.

I kept screaming. The tanker was aimed directly at the centre of our boat. In seconds our home would be splintered. The ship was so close I had to crane my head back to see the top of the bow. I desperately hoped to see a human looking down, a crew member who might witness our boat's destruction and pluck us from the sea if we survived. Instead I saw nothing, apart from streaks of rust below an anchor cinched tight against the hull. The tanker created a surging wave with its bow. This mass of water was about to hit us.

I was still screaming, and Colin was thrashing around in the cabin, trying to turn around so he could see outside. Our boat would be crushed before he even knew what hit him. I grabbed both sides of the hatch, bracing myself for the impact. We rose on the bow wave. But instead of splintering against thousands of tonnes of moving steel, the surge of water pushed us to the freighter's starboard side, and the steel hull slid past, inches from our boat.

Colin finally scrambled around and shoved his head out next to mine. His jaw dropped in disbelief as he stared out at the wall sliding past, still a metre from our boat. The ship was so long—about ninety metres—that it took almost a minute to pass. Waves crashed against the steel, the spray and whitewash deflecting against our own boat. Without another word, Colin ducked back inside the cabin and emerged with the video camera.

I inhaled the acrid scent of combusted diesel and rusting steel, and listened to the not-quite-subsonic rumble of an engine churning out thousands of horsepower. Our own boat rose and fell on the confused seas. A wave could easily slam us into the freighter, fracturing our boat or sucking us through its giant propeller. Then, finally, it was over. The transom of the giant ship passed by, and it continued on its course, oblivious to our existence and our narrowly averted destruction.

"The boat was a foot away from us, I'm not kidding," I said in a shaky voice. "It was coming straight for us."

As the freighter moved on, we stared at the name and home port printed on its stern. *Norca* from Hong Kong would forever be imprinted in our minds. Later research revealed that the steel tanker weighed in at twenty-eight thousand gross tonnes empty—thirty-five thousand times more than our fully loaded boat.

"Thank God our boat is so light and a freighter is so powerful," Colin said. "It takes a lot of force to displace that amount of water. If we were much heavier, the bow wave wouldn't have tossed us to the side so easily."

The irony of that: we'd been saved by our own insignificance. The story might have played out very differently had we been a little farther ahead or the tanker on a slightly different trajectory. If the bow wave had instead pushed us to the portside of the tanker, our drogue line would have been run over and caught on the tanker's hull or propeller. We would have been dragged behind the boat like a forgotten family dog tied to the departing motorhome. We had been very lucky indeed.

These were busy waters. We were parallel to the Strait of Gibraltar, a place where numerous shipping lanes converged. Because of our limited vantage from inside the cabin, we had made a point of regularly opening the hatch and scanning for boats. But from the depths of our trough our outlook was restricted, and even when we crested a wave, neighbouring waves limited our view. We had a radar reflector meant to enhance our signal on other boats' radars. But we had no lofty perch on which to mount the reflector, so it wasn't very effective in high waves. It was terrifying to think that we had been unable to spot an oil tanker, and that its crew had been completely oblivious to us.

Other than our near death, the day was going well. The weather was improving quickly and we ate our first hot meal in two days—rice pudding and coffee. After breakfast, Colin pulled up the drogue and took the first rowing shift while I made our daily water supply.

The technology that enabled us to convert salt water to fresh water was incredible. The desalination unit uses a heavy-duty pump to force salt water past a semi-permeable membrane at high pressure. The pressure creates a process that is the reverse of regular osmosis (where a solute moves from an area of low concentration to an area of high concentration), and fresh water passes through the membrane. The final result is drinkable water with 97 per cent of the salt and minerals extracted.

This sewing-machine-sized desalination unit almost thwarted our journey before it even started. When we received our boat in Lisbon, we discovered our water-maker was defunct. It was an older unit; the malfunction stemmed from leaky seals and problematic valves, which negatively affected the pressurizing mechanism. (If the water cannot be brought to high enough pressure, fresh water is not produced.) The motor whined and groaned, but no fresh water came out. We had two choices: fix it or replace it. We already knew that none of the marine stores sold compact desalinators, so it would have to be shipped in from elsewhere (a process that might take weeks, especially when Portuguese customs was factored in) and would cost five thousand dollars (money we didn't have).

Our only option was to fix it. After countless inquiries and many dead ends, we found a local business that specialized in making gaskets and O-rings, the components we needed. Two bus rides later, I found myself in the industrial section of the city, holding the prized rubber rings in my hand. Meanwhile, Colin had disassembled the unit; when I returned I found him hovering over dozens of meticulously oiled pieces of metal, looking more than a little distressed. Together we cleaned off the various components and replaced the O-rings. We swapped the tired-looking valves with a new set that, by some miracle, we found in the bag that contained the pump manual.

After a full day of tinkering, the desalinator eventually sputtered to life and produced fresh water. I felt a pang of anxiety knowing that we would rely on this decrepit machine to produce enough water to cross an entire ocean. As a precaution—in case our water-maker decided mid-Atlantic to gush gallons through a gimpy gasket—we brought three backup solutions: a small hand-cranked desalinator, a basic still consisting of little more than a pipe, and a rain catchment system.

After just a week at sea, our desalinator performed flawlessly; its electric motor hummed steadily while fresh water trickled forth. After two hours, our ten-litre plastic jug brimmed with clear water that could rival Evian.

We were fervently frugal with our water and used it only for drinking and food preparation. We used salt water for everything else: cleaning, washing, and even cooking noodles and rice (in a diluted solution). Our water-maker was our most treasured piece of equipment, even more precious than the GPS, which sadly did not share its longevity.

"The GPS went out again," Colin said. "Can you try restarting it?"

I pressed the button on our electrical panel to cut its power supply, waited a few seconds, and then turned it on again. "Does that do it?"

"No, I'm still getting that error message that says the antenna connection has shorted."

I leaned out of the cabin and unscrewed the antenna cable from the back of the GPS. It looked okay, but I blew on the terminal anyway to clear any hidden debris before firmly reinserting it. Nothing. Although the unit was brand new, the connection had started to cause problems a few days before, and the short was occurring with increased frequency. Now, no amount of cleaning or fiddling would bring it back to life.

I pulled out our small emergency GPS. It was vastly inferior because it was independently powered and thus could not be left on permanently. Instead, we would turn it on periodically to check that we were still on course. This meant we couldn't continually monitor our speed, which was important for setting the ideal course to accommodate for the variable currents.

The row had been tough so far. We'd lost our drogue, our main GPS had malfunctioned, a tanker almost introduced us to Davy Jones, and we still felt seasick. The experience was very different than my preconceptions, but I wasn't complaining. It seemed a miracle that we were still afloat and still healthy. We were now making good speed, and it appeared our silver lining had finally arrived. The weather continued to improve throughout the day. The winds subsided entirely, but we had a strong, favourable current.

Two birds slightly larger than seagulls soared above us for much of the day. They were white with black shadows near their wingtips and heads. Their flight seemed effortless. With outstretched wings they glided on air currents, a "shearing" flight technique that earned these pelagic birds their name—shearwaters. We now saw only seabirds, and then only two types. The other was the storm petrel, a small black bird with white markings that flew slower and lower to the water than the shearwater.

It was incredible to imagine that these birds spent most of their lives flying above ocean waters. Shearwaters could easily fly a million kilometres in a lifetime. The only thing they couldn't do on the water was breed. For that they would have to travel to a remote island, maybe in the Azores or the Canaries, where the female would lay a single egg in a burrow or rock crevice. But now the two birds I was watching had other priorities: their only concern was the fish they periodically dove into the water for.

THE NEXT FOUR days slipped by quickly while we carried out our routines with pseudo-military precision. If it wasn't for my journal, I could barely distinguish one day from the next, and even these entries were quite brief. The main thing that differentiated the days was what we ate and any sighting for our "I Spy" game.

Colin had started "I Spy." The rule was that you could choose any object on the ocean or in the sky, but nothing on the boat. It may sound lame, but when you're in an unchanging world, the slightest intrusion is exciting. Shearwaters or storm petrels, and sometimes a jumping tuna, were the usual objects. Occasionally it would be a freighter in the distance or a jet contrail. And more often than we liked, we saw a piece of trash float by.

It seemed strange to see garbage so far from land, in such a massive ocean. Where did it come from, where did it go, and who cleaned it up?

According to the 2006 Greenpeace report *Plastic Debris in the World's Oceans*, an estimated 8 million pieces of litter enter the oceans each day. That's 6.4 million tonnes of trash a year. An estimated 20 per cent of that garbage comes from the cargo of ships accidentally lost in storms. The remainder comes from land—trash washed into rivers and storm drains, or offloaded by cities that use the ocean as a de facto landfill site.

We saw at least a piece of trash a day, almost always plastic—a bottle, wrapper, or some other unidentifiable chunk of man-made polymer—which, sadly, was unsurprising, as 90 per cent of the trash floating in the ocean is plastic, according to the 2006 Greenpeace estimate.

This is not good news, because unlike trash in the past, which eventually decomposes, plastic endures. It takes 450 years for a plastic bottle to break down, and what it leaves behind is far from harmless. Unlike natural materials, which decompose into simple chemical components, plastic is synthetic and can't biodegrade. Instead it photodegrades: sunlight breaks it down into smaller and smaller particles. The plastic never leaves the sea; it simply becomes increasingly ingestible, but not digestible. The small, hard polymers still can't be broken down by the wildlife that mistakenly consumes them.

But now there is another danger: the smaller plastic particles absorb non-water-soluble toxins and pesticides, becoming a sponge for DDT and PCBs. The concentration of these chemicals in the plastics is up to one million times higher than in the ocean. In parts of the ocean, plastic outnumbers plankton six to one (in some areas it's as high as one thousand to one), and jellyfish who cannot distinguish between the two consume copious amounts of poisoned plastic particles. The jellyfish are eaten by other animals and the toxins move up the food chain, becoming increasingly concentrated as they accumulate in creatures with longer life spans. At the top of the food chain are whales, which are now so polluted that, when they die and their bodies wash up on shore, some species are treated as toxic waste. Killer whales are the most contaminated species on Earth.

Soon we crossed trash off the list of eligible items for I Spy. It just wasn't fun lying in the cabin guessing bird, plane, or fish while a plastic bucket floated by.

6

A SEA OF MOLTEN METAL

ON OCTOBER 4, our twelfth day at sea, the ocean reached its calmest state yet. The sea gleamed like molten metal as a lazy swell gently rocked our boat. The sky was devoid of clouds. Our little red vessel was the only object that gave us perspective in a vast world of blue.

During my first shift that day, I pulled long, steady strokes on the oars, and I realized that for the first time since leaving Lisbon, I didn't feel seasick. I was ravenous when Colin relieved me at eight, and I wolfed down the meal waiting for me—rice pudding followed by instant coffee laden with full-fat powdered milk. After enjoying one of the most relaxing breakfasts I'd had in a long time, I rinsed my dishes and stowed them under the stove. I exchanged the empty water jug for the full one and turned the desalinator on. As the machine whirred comfortingly, I pulled out a book, shuffled some bags to make a comfortable seat, and began reading.

After a few hours, I glanced at the instrument panel and noticed something was wrong. The amperage meter, which monitors energy inflow from the solar panels, was only showing three amps instead of the usual six at this time of day. With few clouds in the sky, the electrical generation should have been at its peak. Were the solar panels malfunctioning? Perhaps there was a bad connection between the battery and the panels. I groaned inwardly. Our electrical generation system was fundamental; it ran our navigation, communication, and video equipment. And most importantly, it powered our desalination unit.

I clambered onto the deck to see if the solar panels were all right; perhaps they were encrusted in salt and needed cleaning. But I was struck by a bewildering phenomenon. The whole world was dim. It was as though the sun's light had suddenly been obscured by a massive thunderstorm, except the sky was clear.

"What the hell?" I said.

Colin was also looking at the sky, trying to figure out why our world was going dark. "It's a solar eclipse!" he exclaimed excitedly.

I squinted and quickly glanced at the sun; only a large crescent remained. I was amazed. I had seen partial eclipses in the past, viewing them through special glass or, when I was at university, a modified telescope. But I had never seen such a full eclipse. It seemed especially magical since we'd had no idea it was going to take place.

Later we would learn that we just happened to be in one of the best viewing spots in the world for this rare event. It was an annular eclipse, which occurs when the moon is sandwiched by the Earth and sun in such a perfect line that the sun is almost completely blocked. Only a thin halo spills out over the moon's edges, creating a ring of fire. We noticed the eclipse shortly after it began at 8:41 AM in the North Atlantic. We were seven hundred kilometres south of the moon's azimuth, so instead of a ring, we saw a very thin crescent.

Colin stopped rowing, and I climbed on deck. We snapped photographs and marvelled at such celestial beauty. It was not difficult to understand why myths and superstitions accompanied eclipses in previous millennia. The ancient Greeks believed that day turned to night because the gods were angry.

Within the hour, the sun returned to its full glory, and we put it back to work to produce our drinking water.

DURING THIS TRANQUIL period, we kept busy catching up on tasks that were impossible during rougher weather—writing in our journals, taking photographs, organizing the cabin, and one of our most eagerly anticipated chores: retrieving fresh food supplies from the now-accessible deck hatches. Until then, we had relied on a small amount of food stored in an easy-access hatch near the cabin. But that supply was almost gone and, if not for our seasickness-suppressed appetite, would have been consumed days before. Most of our remaining food was stored under the deck, which had been awash during the rough weather.

I pulled out my diagram of the boat's compartments and the list of what was in each of the sixteen holds. The boat's limited space and excessive cargo made it very important to maintain a high level of organization, which quite appealed to the German side of me. I gladly took on the double responsibility of ensuring not only that we could find the chocolate chip cookies, but that we would not eat them all in the first month.

"We'll need to get into all eight round hatches," I said, gazing at the drawing. "The square hatches under the rowing seat have food for the second half of the trip, so we can give them a miss."

Colin stopped rowing and pulled the oars on deck. We stuffed blocks of closed-cell foam—cut out from one of our fenders—into the scuppers to prevent water from flowing onto the deck and into the open hatches. I read out the desired bounty from the list, and Colin retrieved it. The food piled up in the cabin: a bag of rice, six apples, a pouch of dehydrated potatoes, a box of tapioca, five sachets of pudding, two cans of green beans...Thankfully, very little water had leaked into the starboard compartments.

But at the fourth hatch, Colin reached in, grimaced, and pulled out handfuls of bloated, dripping pasta. The hatch was full of water. Some of the food was in sealed cans, but much of it wasn't. We had lost ten kilograms of precious noodles— half of all our pasta—and a bag of flour. Although we still had rice, dried bread, and dehydrated potatoes, we'd lost a significant portion of our carbohydrate supply. The cans exposed to the corrosive salt water were quickly rusting, so we would have to use them soon. The rest of our compartments had fared better, although some of our lemons and cabbages had started to rot from dampness, leaving a horrific smell. The malodour of the cabbage was especially pervasive, and even after we tossed the rotting vegetable over the side and washed the compartment with bleach, the smell lingered for the remainder of our Atlantic crossing. We lovingly called this compartment the "cabbage cupboard."

We had budgeted for two hot meals a day, breakfast and dinner. Lunch was a variation on sandwiches: dried breads with meat, cheese, peanut butter or jam. The first meal of the day was pudding or porridge followed by instant coffee, both heavily loaded with full-fat milk powder. We rotated between rice pudding, oatmeal, semolina, and tapioca, with caramel, banana, or vanilla pudding mix sometimes added in. My favourite was tapioca; Colin preferred vanilla rice pudding. For special occasions, we had pancakes with whipped cream that came in small Tetra Paks. Dinner was a carbohydrate, such as instant mashed potatoes or rice, and a protein (usually canned tuna or canned beef stew), with canned vegetables on the side every other night.

The calm weather continued into the next day, and we persisted with overdue chores. Colin did several phone interviews with newspapers back home and wrote in his journal. We wrote an update for our website and dictated it to Dean Fenwick, our de facto home-base coordinator, who in turn read out e-mails people had sent us. We called our parents. I poured vegetable oil over Colin's hair and worked out two massive dreadlocks. We lathered ourselves up with buckets of water and rinsed with quick dips in the ocean—quick because of the danger of sharks and because of our rigorous rowing schedule.

Things were starting to take on a sense of normalcy. We'd wake up at 6:00 AM and row until 2:00 AM. I had the first shift, Colin the last. Colin made breakfast and I prepared dinner. Lunch was fend-for-yourself. We brushed our teeth twice a day and bathed when we could. Despite cramped quarters and round-the-clock slave labour, we fell into comfortable routines, and I couldn't help but marvel at the ability

85

of humans to adapt to extreme conditions. Around the world, people have learned to cope with temperatures from minus fifty degrees Celsius to plus forty. Homes are made out of whatever material is at hand, whether snow, mud, straw, or leaves. And now Colin and I had finally adapted to life in a quarter-inch plywood rowboat in the middle of the ocean.

Back in Canada, while researching our proposed voyage, I had contacted several ocean rowers. I clearly remember the words of one cynical rower from Britain who offered this advice to help me envision the ocean rowing experience: "Climb under your kitchen table and don't come out again for three months." I had laughed at the time, but now I was realizing how true this statement was. It takes time for the mind to adjust to such a bizarre reality. I felt my mind simplifying in order to cope with the small world we lived in. Basic things like eating a cookie or watching a colourful sunset gave me immense pleasure. I found it intriguing how differently identical experiences can be perceived, depending on mood and environment.

Now I couldn't help but reassess my needs. What did I really need in life? What was most important to me? What made me happy? It seemed strange that, despite such a precarious existence, all I needed to be content was some food in my stomach and calm weather. I wasn't sure if my sudden inner peace was a result of removing the complexities of life in civilization, or if it was the same happiness that comes when the hammer stops pounding your cranium. After all, for the first ten days, I had been miserable, scared, seasick, and malnourished. Regardless, I now felt pleased with our new lifestyle and no longer dreaded the expanse that lay ahead of us.

One of the reasons I like long self-propelled journeys is because they help me to view the world and myself differently. I don't know whether it's the lack of distractions, the rigorous exercise, or the new experiences, but I come away from these journeys wiser and happier. I thought back to when I was trekking through the Annapurna mountain range in Nepal. A young boy had ran up to me and asked, "Why are you travelling alone, where are your friends? I will walk with you." As we walked through the villages, he waved to everyone he saw, saying, "That is my sister, that is my aunt," and so on. For the Nepalese, as in many less developed countries, family is the centre of their existence. Families live together, work together, and eat together. No one has a four-figure salary, car, or home with appliances, but they do have a very strong sense of community.

While Colin rowed and I daydreamed, I suddenly noticed a shape in the distance.

"What's that?" I said.

Colin paused on the oars and squinted in the direction I was pointing. "What?"

"It's gone now, but I think I saw a fin," I said.

"Was it a shark?"

"I'm not sure. It was quite big."

I peered into the depths looking for any sign of the animal, but saw nothing.

Colin had a distant look in his eyes, and I knew he was about to reflect on his sailing days, "I actually knew of a boat that was attacked by a sha . . . "

PHHHHHHHHAAAAAART

A sudden exhalation, like the airbrakes on a semi, made me jump. Colin fell right off the rowing seat in fright and rolled onto the deck. A shower of spray shot into the air six metres away from us.

Between bursts of laughter, I managed to squeak out, "It's a whale."

Another burst of spray shot into the air and the unmistakable odour of foul fish wafted our way. The whale's back rose out of the water like a submarine surfacing. The mammal was dark grey and looked to be about six metres long. We watched in awe as it swam next to us, though I was a little concerned at its close proximity. But Colin assured me that all whales are excellent navigators (they use both sight and sonar) and that the chances of it mistakenly hitting our boat were very low. After an all-too-short visit, it dove under our boat and disappeared into the depths for good.

"I think that was a minke whale," I said excitedly, flipping through the pages of our guidebook. I knew that minke whales lived in these waters and that this whale was relatively small and narrow, which is typical of the species. "They're the second-smallest baleen whales; adults are on average seven metres long and weigh five tonnes," I said after looking in our guidebook. "They may be small by whale standards, but they're about the length of our boat and six times as heavy." The ocean is the only environment on Earth where animals can grow to such proportions.

Minke whales have earned themselves the unfortunate but appropriate nickname "stinky minke" among whale watchers. Their halitosis stems in part from their astounding ability to hold their breath for up to twenty minutes, allowing them to dive to great depths in search of food. They eat tiny shrimp-like creatures called krill as well as other crustaceans and fish. To catch prey, the minke whale has hundreds of baleen plates that hang down from the roof of its mouth. The baleen plates work like a sieve, filtering its meal from the copious amount of water that passes through its mouth.

The minke whale is known for being curious towards boats, and it generally travels solo unless it is in feeding grounds. Our visitor was most likely a northern minke, which inhabits much of the Northern Hemisphere and has a distinguishing white band on its flippers.

The minke's small size is partially responsible for its relative abundance, as it has made them of little value to large-scale whaling operations in the past. Ironically, their name immortalizes the inept Norwegian whaler Miencke, who accidentally harpooned one instead of the coveted blue whale. Minkes weren't desirable to whalers when their larger counterparts, such as the blue, were plentiful, but that has changed as those populations have declined and restrictions were implemented. The International Whaling Commission, a governing body that protects whale populations, established a moratorium on commercial whaling in 1986. Nonetheless, a quick browse through the reports on the IWC website shows that minke whales continue to be hunted for different reasons: in Japan for scientific purposes and in Greenland for aboriginal sustenance. Anti-whaling groups are critical of some of these practices. In 2007 the WWF published a report titled *Japanese Scientific Whaling: Irresponsible Science, Irresponsible Whaling* that concluded, "Overall, the scientific research conducted by Japan is nothing more than a plan designed to keep the whaling fleet in business." But others argue that minke whale populations are robust. Norway, for instance, resumed whaling in 1993, and its embassy website states that minke whaling is an "environmentally sound means of food production."

I hoped our spouting friend would have a long life and that its visit would mark the start of regular visits by other marine mammals and fish. We had seen very little wildlife in the sea, whereas just a few decades ago, adventurers who had crossed oceans in similarly slow-moving boats—such as John Fairfax in his ocean rowboat or Thor Heyderdahl in his *Kon-Tiki* raft—had seen whales, dolphins, turtles, sharks, and fish on a regular basis. It certainly felt as though I was observing the declining biodiversity of our world's oceans with my own eyes.

The whale didn't stay as long as we would have liked, and soon we were alone again. But our solitude wasn't lengthy.

"There's a boat coming towards us," Colin said.

"Well, get some clothes on," I said. "I'm sure that whoever they are, they're not going to enjoy seeing your hairy ass."

I tossed Colin a pair of shorts through the hatch and he stopped rowing to pull them on. I wiggled into my swimsuit. We had stopped wearing clothes because of salt sores. Continual spray from the ocean made our clothes unbearably salty, and the fabric chafed our skin. With limited fresh water, we couldn't wash our clothes. The only solution was to abandon clothing altogether. The salt sores had disappeared, but I worried we were being exposed to far too much UV radiation. The sunscreen we applied several times throughout the day seemed to wear off much too quickly from sweat and waves to be able to contend with the intense subtropical sun.

I craned my head through the hatch and watched as a small ship approached our vessel. A line of crew members stood against the rail looking towards us, making it obvious they were not on a collision course. A rumbling diesel propelled the wooden vessel, which looked like a fishboat. Two dogs barked excitedly, tails wagging; they looked as though they were about to jump over the side.

"*Buenos días*," a man yelled from the wheelhouse.

"*Hola*," Colin responded, casually continuing to row.

Our craft looked very similar to a lifeboat, and several freighters had already radioed to ask if we needed assistance. This crew of salty fishermen probably thought we were a couple of castaways. We did our best to look and sound like two people nonchalantly and purposely rowing across the ocean.

"*Bonita día*," I yelled, not even sure if I was speaking in Spanish.

The man in the wheelhouse fired a series of incomprehensible questions while he steered the boat in circles around us.

I smiled and pointed to their boat. "*Español?*"

"*Sí.*"

When the captain realized we were not in distress, his face broke into a broad grin. "*Loco, loco.*"

I turned on the video camera and emerged from the cabin to film our visitors. By now they had gotten over their bewilderment, and the entire crew burst into applause. They excitedly shouted unintelligible questions. We must have been quite a sight to these hardened fishermen. I looked like a typical bikini-clad tourist, while Colin sported the beard and wild hair of a castaway. When we managed to explain that we were bound for Miami, another bout of cheers erupted. After more hand-waving and barely comprehensible exchanges, they left and we were alone again.

OUR NEXT VISITORS were even more unusual. I was rowing when I saw what looked like a housefly buzzing over the stern of the boat. It landed on the railing, took a few steps, and then flew to another part of the boat. This would seem perfectly normal if we were tied up at the dock, but the nearest land was four hundred kilometres away. I wondered whether it had been with us the whole time, but that didn't seem likely. I puzzled over how it had ended up so far away from land.

Later that day we saw a small white moth and another fly (or perhaps the same one). A hoverfly and a dragonfly appeared the following day. We couldn't understand it. The nearest land was the northwestern tip of Africa, but it was hundreds of kilometres away. Insects rarely fly ten kilometres from shore, let alone four hundred. We theorized that perhaps an unusual meteorological wave had swept them high into the troposphere and deposited them over the ocean.

A few other things seemed different, too. The sky was a kaleidoscope of alternating cloud formations, rapidly changing from cirrocumulus, to cumulonimbus, and then to stratus. The sun burned red and unnatural. And without a breeze, the air was muggy and oppressive. The currents had also stopped, and the ocean became a pool of mercury with an oily swell that lifted and dropped our boat so gently that it didn't rock. Even though I enjoyed rowing on such a smooth surface, something seemed almost sinister about the lifeless, overheated state of the ocean.

Colin seemed unconcerned, and I took comfort from the statistics offered by the pilot charts. Our latitude was now low enough that we wouldn't be affected by the fall and winter tempests that form off Europe. We were, in fact, in an area of the Atlantic Ocean that almost never has storms of any sort through the fall. And, of course, we were still thousands of kilometres from the eastern edge of the hurricane belt.

THE MORNING OF October 8 marked our seventeenth day rowing and my thirty-first birthday. Instead of our usual breakfast of oatmeal or rice pudding, Colin undertook the laborious task of making pancakes. We had no syrup on board, so he caramelized sugar in a pan above the single burner and added a splash of water. A scent more like fresh doughnuts than pancakes filled the boat. I peered into the galley and noticed my chef was cooking the pancakes in a quarter-inch of oil. He was deep-frying them! He then topped the crisp, golden morsels with syrup, strawberry jam, and some of the whipped cream from the Tetra Paks. Then Colin stacked the finished product on a plate, topped it with a candle, and sang the full chorus of "Happy Birthday."

"You shouldn't have," I crooned, not meaning a single word of it, before blowing out the candle.

"Did you make a wish?"

"Of course, but I'm not telling you, otherwise it won't come true."

I had wished for better winds. The previous day the winds had started to blow from the south, which, according to our pilot charts, was quite rare. At first the winds had been very light, but the night before the headwinds had strengthened to force three and our progress had ground to a halt. Now the contrary winds were even stronger, and the waves had grown to nearly two metres. It looked like it would be another day without rowing, another day stuck in the cabin, slowly drifting backwards.

Faced with a tower of pancakes, I momentarily forgot my disappointment. I dug my fork into the scrumptious, crispy pile of sugar, flour, and grease. Now that we were over our seasickness, food had reached an almost godly status. It was our reward, a distraction, a moment of bliss in a difficult day.

"Mmmm, thank you," I murmured.

"These are good," Colin enthused. "And there's still more to your birthday celebration; wait until tonight's dinner."

"It's a date."

When the excitement of my birthday breakfast was over, we climbed back into the cabin to ride out the heavy headwinds. The day dragged by. It was too rough to read, so we whiled away the time telling each other stories from the past. Colin regaled me with tales from his days sailing alone in the Pacific. He told me about his parrot named Pirate, and about how he had climbed coconut trees, gone spear-fishing, and sailed through storms. While Colin was adventuring and trying to spread his DNA—albeit without biological intentions— I had been at university studying genetics. As our rowboat drifted slowly backwards, I told Colin about life at universities in Hamilton, Victoria, and England. Our conversations swung from the past to the future. We talked about the home we would buy one day and about all the meals we would cook in the kitchen—Thai coconut lemongrass curry, eggplant in black bean sauce, deep-fried bananas with coconut ice cream...

"Do you feel that?" Colin suddenly asked.

"Feel what?"

"I'm not quite sure. It's kind of like a subsonic sound— you can't quite hear it, but you just know it's there—maybe through the vibration on your skin," Colin said, cocking his head as if to improve his hearing. "But it's not sound, it's more like pressure—fluctuating air pressure," he added, looking slightly puzzled.

"No, I can't say I do. I do have a slight headache. I think it's caused by the heat, combined with your farts."

Colin didn't answer this with the wisecrack I expected. Instead he had a slight frown of concentration.

"I'm going to check for boats again. Maybe it's the rumble of a diesel I'm feeling," Colin said.

He opened the hatch, climbed outside, and stood for about five minutes, ducking on occasion to avoid spray coming over the boat. Finally he returned to the cabin.

"Nothing. We're definitely alone on the sea right now. You know, there's something really weird about this weather. I wish we had a barometer. And what about all these bugs we've been seeing flying around? During my years sailing, I never saw insects this far from land," Colin said.

I ran my fingers through his greasy, salt-encrusted hair. "Don't worry, honey. I'm sure it's nothing. We're just getting a couple days of headwinds. Soon it will all go back to normal. I bet we'll be able to row again by this evening."

As the day wore on, my optimistic words rang empty. The headwinds picked up and, by evening, conditions were so rough that Colin had to cancel the romantic birthday dinner he had planned. Instead, we had crackers, cheese, and a chunk of dry meat.

The following morning we were greeted by an awesome spectacle. As the sun lifted above the horizon, the sky turned a red so vibrant that it looked like an accident in Photoshop.

But I couldn't help feeling concerned, even as I looked at such a beautiful sunrise. There was no story Colin liked to regale me with more than the reliability of the ancient expression, "Red sky in the morning, sailors take warning."

Versions of this proverb have been in existence since biblical times. (In Matthew XVI, Jesus says, "When it is evening, ye say, it will be fair weather: for the sky is red. And in the morning, it will be foul weather today: for the sky is red and lowering.") The colours we see in the sky depend on the composition of the atmosphere. When the atmosphere is packed with water vapour and dust, only the longest wavelength, red, penetrates the particulate and is visible. The shorter blue wavelengths are scattered and less apparent. In the evenings and mornings, the sun sits low on the horizon and transmits light through the thickest part of the atmosphere. A red sky therefore means more dust and water in the air. Since storms tend to move more from west to east (predominant wind directions play a role in this), red at night means the storm has passed and a high-pressure system is moving in, while in the morning, red announces an arriving tempest.

We spent the day in discomfort. My nightly journal entry was tellingly brief: "Too rough and contrary winds to row. Lost the second and final drogue. The swivel broke. Left the chain and rope in the water—hopefully it'll have some effect." The winds and waves had continued to build throughout the day and, without the sea anchor, we were even more at the mercy of the waves. It was too rough to cook, and running the desalinator was impossible. We had nothing to do but wait. We lay in the cabin, uncomfortable, hot, sore, and nauseous. Our chores were reduced to keeping watch and pumping out the bilge. Occasionally, we opened one of the hatches in the cabin, which was airtight and made it not only hot but suffocating.

How long does it take to develop bedsores? I wondered. I felt like I had been lying in this cabin for years. I slipped in and out of dreamless sleep, wishing for time to speed up. The bad weather continued to escalate and, by the time night arrived, the winds blew at what we estimated was fifty kilometres per hour. The winds had changed direction gradually, and were now coming from the west. Confused waves seemed to come from multiple directions, occasionally colliding to send a column of water into the air.

The waves looked like they had grown overnight, and we guessed the conditions were now force eight. Our boat lay in disarray. We were being beaten into a semi-comatose state of submission. Waves shuffled the contents of our cabin; cracker crumbs and milk powder dusted us, and water leaking through the roof saturated us and everything else inside. I could barely remember how it felt to stretch my legs. When we lay down, which was most of the time, agitated seas rubbed our heads against the mattress. My hair had become an oversized dreadlock, and Colin's was even wilder-looking. This was our third day of cabin confinement, and it did not seem like relief was around the corner. In the afternoon, I mustered the energy to make a phone call. I took the satellite phone from its waterproof case, positioned the antenna near the hatch for the best reception, and dialled my Dad's number. I thanked God, or more accurately, the technical genius of Iridium satellite telephones, for the ability to call home from the mid-Atlantic. As the phone rang, I imagined my father getting off the couch in his suburban Toronto home and padding across the living room to pick up the handset.

"Hello," he said, right on cue.

"Hi Dad, it's me," I said, happy to hear his voice. "Things are going well, and we've made it almost eight hundred kilometres from Lisbon..."

My father cut me off. "Honey, things *aren't* going well. I just heard on the news that the most northeastern hurricane in history has formed—Hurricane Vince. I looked up its coordinates on the National Hurricane Center website, and it's only six hundred kilometres away from you."

I was stunned. Maybe there was a mistake. "Which direction is it heading?" I finally asked.

My father was silent for several seconds before he replied, "Straight towards you."

7

OUR FIRST
HURRICANE

OW COULD THIS be happening to us? It wasn't right; it
wasn't fair. Never in history had there been a hurricane on this area of the Atlantic, and even the likelihood of a regular storm at this time of year was low. Why now?
Was it global warming, natural weather quirks, or just bad
luck? Was it something I did? Perhaps it was Nature's way of
saying: *You wanted to experience the ocean? Well, here it is.*

Asking why didn't help our situation. My one hope was
that my father was mistaken—perhaps he had misread the
news report or assumed we were elsewhere. I decided to get
verification and called my friend Mary. Her delight in hearing from me evaporated as she relayed the latest information
on Hurricane Vince from the website of the National Hurricane Center, a government-run organization that monitors
and predicts hurricane activity in the Atlantic Ocean from
its base in Florida. Hurricane Vince had formed several hundred kilometres away from us in a part of the ocean thought

to be too cold to support hurricanes. The Hurricane Center stated it was the most northeastern hurricane in history, a complete anomaly. The worst part was that Vince was tracking straight towards us, just as my dad had said.

Colin and I stared at each other in shock. A heavy silence was punctuated only by the raucous roar of waves and the dishevelling impact that followed. I just wanted to close my eyes and pretend this wasn't happening.

"Do you know what my birthday wish was?" I asked, finally breaking the silence.

"What?"

"For better winds," I said, trying to hold back my tears and anger at the irony of it. "All I wanted was for the headwinds to stop."

"Wow, it's like some evil entity pricked up its ears when you said that. I thought those clouds looked peculiar, but I didn't want to worry you. See those rows of wispy ones?" Colin said, pointing to high clouds that looked like white unfurled cotton candy. "They're cirrus—quite rare to see on the ocean, except before a big storm." Before this we had seen mostly cumulus, big puffy white clouds that begged you to find shapes in them.

"So I guess that nice weather we had a few days ago was just the calm before the storm," I said.

From the Hurricane Center we found out that three days before, on October 6, when we had been revelling in pleasantly calm conditions, a frontal low from the northwest had swept over the Azores Islands seven hundred kilometres to the northwest. Meteorologists called it occluded and deep-layer; the wave of low pressure had brought thunderstorms and foul weather. Over the next two days, the storm had intensified and, on October 8, just as I was waking up and looking forward to celebrating my birthday, it became a subtropical storm. At that point the unusually placid waters we'd been experiencing were forming ripples from a stiffening westerly breeze, but we still thought little of the change. Tropical Storm Vince continued to intensify, and when winds speeds reached 120 kilometres per hour, it became a hurricane.

The formation of a hurricane in the cool waters above the Canary Islands seemed impossible. According to the National Hurricane Center, the temperature of these waters was only 23 to 24 degrees Celsius; hurricanes are generally thought to need surface temperatures of at least 26.5 degrees Celsius to form. The Hurricane Center doubted the likelihood of a hurricane so much that they held off a full day before bestowing Vince with his name (only cyclonic storms are named). In a written discussion dated October 9, it stated, "if it looks like a hurricane... it probably is... despite its environment and unusual location."

For most people, the fact that Vince was a freak was nothing more than academic. Newspapers around the world used this interesting tidbit to fill tight spaces between ads. The most northeasterly-forming hurricane in history made for a catchy headline. But all the articles stressed that there was nothing to worry about; it was far out at sea. *The Edmonton Journal* reassured readers with its story "Hurricane's No Danger to the U.S."

But for two Canadians in a quarter-inch-thick plywood rowboat sitting directly in the hurricane's path, Vince definitely was a danger.

It was surreal to look through the salt-crusted Plexiglas hatch at the spirited waves slapping our boat. The ocean conditions were still reasonable, but the new information set off an emotional tempest in our hearts and minds. A storm with the strength of a ten-megatonne nuclear bomb exploding every twenty minutes was moving implacably towards us across the open ocean. I felt like a prisoner in a penitentiary about to be consumed by flames. There was no way out. All we could do was sit in our tiny cabin and hope we would survive. I tried to calm myself through rationalization and ponder how we could prepare for the storm. Really, though, I felt the chances were quite high that we wouldn't survive, if the hurricane hit us square on.

"Well, I guess we'd better clear the decks and get all our safety equipment as handy as possible," Colin said in a flat voice. "We can move the life raft a little closer to the entrance hatch, at the expense of some shoulder space."

"Have you noticed that we haven't seen any ships since that fishing boat four days ago?" I said. Before then, the seas had been quite busy, and usually we saw several freighters each day.

"Yeah, undoubtedly all shipping is being routed away from the hurricane's path," Colin said. "I strongly suspect we're the last boat in this neck of the woods."

We clambered onto the deck and began readying it for the storm ahead. We double-checked the lashing of the spare oars and stowed the working oars. We removed the stove from its plywood recess and stuffed it into the adjacent locker. We double-checked the bilge pump, made sure all hatches were secured properly, removed and secured the rudder, and coiled loose ropes. Finally, Colin and I returned to the cabin, dripping with ocean spray, and began preparing it. We nailed down all the plywood lids for the compartments beneath our bed. This would prevent the huge mass of food and equipment stored beneath the mattress from becoming a lethal avalanche if the boat capsized.

Colin checked the batteries in the handheld VHF radio and GPS, and I organized our emergency supplies. We had a grab bag that contained what we'd need if we were forced to abandon ship and climb into the life raft. This yellow dry bag held flares, a handheld VHF radio, a GPS, high-energy food, a small amount of drinking water, the hand-crank desalinator, a signalling mirror, a small first aid kit, and other important items for survival. I added some additional chocolate, and then, thinking back to Colin's earlier story about the crew member on the capsized trimaran and her baseball-sized turd, tossed in a handful of prunes.

Once the boat was ready, we went through verbal drills for different disasters. We would abandon the rowboat only if it was completely destroyed. If the boat was holed or taking in water, we would fight to stop the inflow and then bail or pump out the brine. If we capsized, we would wait for the boat to right and, if it didn't, we would sway our bodies back and forth in unison to rock it back upright.

I called the Hurricane Center for an update, praying that Vince had changed course or dissipated. They relayed Vince's coordinates, speed, and predicted path. The news was not good. The hurricane was still moving towards us and the eye was now only four hundred kilometres away. We could expect the weather conditions to degrade significantly, and within twenty-four hours, we would be in the centre of the storm.

I plotted the hurricane's present position on the chart, and it looked frighteningly close to the little X that marked our position. I still struggled to comprehend the significance that these markings represented. One X was a small plywood rowboat, our home. The X with the circle around it was a full-fledged hurricane. We were already in the perimeter of the hurricane, and it was predicted to keep moving towards us at twenty kilometres per hour.

I peered out the hatch. Suddenly, the sea was formidable, savagely powerful. All around us, the waters heaved and surged. The crests of giant aqueous mountains collapsed in great foaming avalanches. Winds blasted spray and foam horizontally across the sea's surface. It had only taken a few hours for the sea to transform from moderate swell to total chaos. This morning the winds had been force seven on the Beaufort scale, which would have elicited a small craft warning. Now they had intensified to force nine—gale-force. We could expect conditions to escalate to force twelve or greater (off the scale) when the hurricane was on top of us.

These conditions were beyond anything I had imagined before embarking on this expedition. I couldn't even begin to conceptualize the state of the ocean in a force-twelve storm. Already conditions inside our boat were unbearable. Colin and I slammed against each other with every breaking wave. I was bruised and in pain. My seasickness had returned, and I was unable to eat or drink.

I broke the silence and articulated the question that hung over us. "How bad do you think it's going to get?"

Colin looked more worried than I had ever seen. "I once had two cyclones simultaneously heading towards my sailboat in the Coral Sea in 1997—cyclones Harold and Gillian..."

I had already heard this story, but now I listened with a renewed, grim fascination. Colin had been en route to Papua New Guinea from Australia when he heard on the shortwave radio that not one but two cyclones were forming on the Coral Sea. Neither of the storms had hit him square on, but his boat sustained significant damage and he barely made it through. He and two Danish backpackers he had taken on as crew bailed the boat throughout the storm using buckets after their bilge pump broke. They had barely kept the boat from sinking.

"I expect it will be a lot worse than that, and that was bad," Colin said. "After that final sailing voyage in 1997, I vowed never to sail in a cyclone zone again."

He exhaled a long, deep sigh. He looked defeated. "But here I am once again, sitting in a small boat with a hurricane closing in."

Although the malevolent clouds and torrential rain already blocked most of the sun's glow, I became terrified when all the light from our shadowy world was extinguished at 6:30 PM. I felt I was in a coffin and somebody had just closed the lid for the last time. According to all reports, the hurricane's strength would be at its peak shortly after midnight. If disaster struck, we would have to function in complete darkness. I shivered and squeezed Colin close.

The wind created a permanent high-pitched shriek as it whipped through the lifelines. Breaking waves roared and gurgled—at times sounding almost guttural, like the voices of old men. I wished for my earplugs to block out the sounds. Giant waves slammed into the boat, launching us sideways down their faces at frightening speeds. Sometimes our vessel was pushed onto its side as it catapulted forward. Inside the cabin we smashed against the thinly padded walls and each other. I was tired, exhausted, and scared. I needed time to rest and recover, but the ocean wouldn't allow it.

It was now 9:00 PM and the cabin was completely dark, except for the bright flashes of our strobe light and the frequent lightning strikes. I tucked my head into the narrow stern and felt Colin's feet pressed against my neck. Lying head to foot seemed safer because it gave us each room to brace ourselves for the impact of the waves. I listened intently to the ocean, trying to discern the size of the waves from the thunderous bellows that heralded their approach.

The biggest waves were always preceded by a moment of silence, as though they sucked the life from the neighbouring swells to gain their power. While Colin struggled to secure the life raft that had come free of its mounting, a sudden quiet caught me by surprise. The only noise was the incessant shrieking of the wind. Even the boat had momentarily stopped moving. Suddenly our boat began rising, and I could hear a deep rumbling that quickly increased in intensity. Instinctively I knew this would be the biggest hit yet, and I braced my shoulders against both sides of the boat. A small squeak of terror escaped my lips.

An intense force threw the boat onto its side while water surged over the deck and cabin. We landed on the starboard wall, and I could feel Colin's teeth digging into my feet. The life raft, encased in a hard plastic shell, had slammed into his back and was pinning him momentarily against my legs and the wall. The boat teetered for a few seconds on its side, and I was sure we were going over. A second explosive wave hit the boat and, thankfully, knocked it upright.

I pulled the life raft away from Colin and was relieved to see he was all right. We worked quickly to lash it down before it caused real damage. A loose fifty-two-kilogram object inside the boat's cabin was dangerous and I wasn't in the mood to appreciate the irony of being killed by our life raft.

"It's 2:00 AM," Colin said. "This is when the storm was supposed to peak."

Although the hurricane's force was far from over, this was excellent news; we would have to wait only a few more hours before conditions started to subside. I patted the wooden walls of our boat and quietly thanked her. When I had first laid eyes on *Ondine*, I'd had a good feeling about her. I now felt that she would take us through to the other side of Hurricane Vince.

I was still tired, but most of my fear had been replaced with guilt. I felt terrible for all the worry I caused my parents. It was my decision to be here and I accepted the risks, but my parents didn't have a choice in the matter. They had raised me in a protective environment, but now that I was an adult, they could only voice their displeasure at my life choices and eventually accept them. Every time I spoke to my mom, she'd say, in parting, "I pray for you every night." It gave her piece of mind that I was in God's benevolent hands (except she worried I wouldn't go to heaven because I wasn't Lutheran). I don't know if my dad prayed for me, but he did tell me that I had given him more than a few grey hairs and sleepless nights.

When Colin was rowing across the Bering Sea nine months before I joined him in Moscow, I realized just how difficult it is to be at home while the one you love is in danger. The Bering Sea contains some of the world's most dangerous waters, and conditions were so severe that the U.S. Coast Guard requested I relay Colin's coordinates to them twice a day. With nothing to do but wait, I felt powerless. That horrendous feeling influenced my decision to row across the Atlantic. Instead of helplessly waiting and worrying while Colin rowed across the Atlantic as part of his circumnavigation of the world, I wanted to be absorbed by my own exciting challenge. And although I could think of a million places I'd rather have been now, if Colin was facing this hurricane, I didn't want to be anywhere else. At least whatever happened would happen to both of us.

I prayed we would be able to endure the storm and watch the rising sun, but my words felt hollow, directed to a nebulous, omnipotent being I didn't fully believe in. For me, religion has always been a source of confusion and disruption. As a child, each of my parents tried to convince me of the merits of their respective religions, Islam and Lutheranism. I went to a Catholic high school because my parents worried the public school was crowded with hoodlums. I attended church, mosque, Sunday school, and Islamic teachings. I was baptized, and I owned a prayer rug, a head scarf, a robe, the Koran, and the Bible.

I didn't mind learning about different religions, but I loathed the strife and turmoil they caused in our home. My parents fought bitterly about religion and how I should be raised. My mother slyly served my father pork while my father scolded my mother for not converting to Islam. "A Muslim man must have a Muslim wife," he'd say. "What's wrong with pork?" my mother would ask. She just couldn't understand why he wouldn't eat a nice German bratwurst or schnitzel. And I couldn't understand how something that was supposed to promote peace and love could foster such insensitivity and animosity.

My parents tried hard to make things work, but I knew from an early age that they stayed together mostly for me. So when I was fourteen and my dad told me he was divorcing my mom, I wasn't surprised. In a way, it was almost a relief, an unburdening of guilt stemming from my belief that I'd caused my parents to sacrifice so much of their lives to a relationship that made them unhappy.

My mom seemed to take the news fairly well. It wasn't a traumatic affair—she just accepted it, and the divorce was more of a slow transition. My mom and I continued living on the Trenton base in military housing, while my dad moved to Oshawa, a city an hour and a half away, and remarried. My mom and I eventually moved into low-income housing in Trenton, and after I left for university, she relocated to Hamilton, where she still lives now. Meanwhile, my father went through another divorce and now lives in Toronto, married to a sweet Syrian woman with whom he has two lovely children.

BY 6:00 AM THE energy of the storm had decreased noticeably. The rays of the rising sun pierced through tattered holes in sullen clouds, illuminating spray that glittered as it was driven by forty-five-knot winds. Small rainbows formed and vanished, a moving kaleidoscope of colour.

"I think we've done it," I whispered. "We've made it through the hurricane. Just a few more hours and things should be getting better."

Colin nodded. His eyes were bloodshot, and his body was marked with bruises. I'm sure I looked no better. I had just experienced the worst three days of my life. But now, the prospect of the hurricane passing provided immense relief. I rolled onto the sweat-soaked duvet and snuggled my head into the pillow. For the first time in two days, I fell into a deep, peaceful sleep.

8

THROUGH THE
CANARY ISLANDS

THREE IRREGULARLY coloured clouds sat on the horizon. They were white and puffy on top, but dark grey underneath. They sat stationary in an otherwise clear sky. Despite their unusual colour, I wasn't worried. In fact, I was quite excited by the presence of these clouds. Before the era of Global Positioning Systems and accurate charts, mariners relied on clouds to indicate land in the distance. That's because warm air above ground rises to build clouds.

Since the passing of Hurricane Vince two weeks before, we had encountered fair weather conditions and made good progress towards the Canary Islands, two hundred kilometres off the shores of Morocco. We had not seen land since leaving Portugal almost a month before, and were excited at the prospect of viewing volcanic mountains rising from the sea. Our GPS indicated that the islands were still about a hundred kilometres away. These puffs in the distance had likely formed over the Canaries, and it was somewhat reassuring to have a natural verification of land in the distance, not just a digital readout.

I looked for other signs of land that the ancient mariners had relied upon. Were distant islands interrupting the pattern of the waves? I couldn't really see any significant changes. I looked for non-pelagic birds in the sky, but just saw the usual shearwaters and stormy petrels. Recently, however, we had witnessed more bountiful wildlife in the sea. Yesterday had been particularly lively and we'd spotted a pod of more than fifty dolphins, a six-metre whale, a much smaller shark, and a hawksbill turtle. The Canary Islands are a world-class diving destination, and it made sense that the density of marine life would increase as we neared the shallow waters off the reefs.

I frequently peered over my shoulder as I pulled the oars through the relatively calm waters, anxious to catch my first glimpse of land again. The visibility wasn't great because of a haze. At the end of my shift, as I stood up to get off the rowing seat, my increased vantage point allowed me to see farther into the distance. I could see a faint blue smudge rising from the sea, and I knew it wasn't a cloud.

"It's land!" I shouted.

Colin climbed out of the cabin, peered into the distance, and gave a whoop of excitement. We both stood on the deck, staring in awe at terra firma in the distance. When Hurricane Vince had borne down on us two weeks ago, I thought I might never see land again. Now, ensconced in a settled high-pressure system and stable weather, Colin and I entered the waters off the Canary Islands. I felt I had finally emerged from a very dark dream. I longed to set foot on solid ground again.

Tempting as it was, we had no plans of making landfall in the Canary Islands. The danger of landing on these islands, which are buttressed with high cliffs and crashing waves, was just too great. We couldn't risk losing our boat on the rocks. Instead, we would stay well away from their churning shorelines as we passed between them. It would still be reassuring to be near civilization.

As the islands became more distinct, we could make out the two most eastern islands of the group, Lanzarote and Fuerteventura. Rocky beige slopes reached for the sea and volcanic cinder cones stretched skyward to create a pocked landscape. These two islands are the driest in the Canary archipelago, and the little rainfall they receive keeps their slopes devoid of greenery. There are no year-round streams on any on the islands; instead, a network of ravines occasionally drains rainwater and, at the higher elevations, snowmelt.

A large variety of animals make their home on the Canary Islands—including, not surprisingly, canaries. But the islands were not named after the bird. The ancient Romans encountered fierce dogs on one of the islands. They deemed the place *Insula Canaria*—Latin for "Island of the Dogs." Eventually the name Canary came to be used to describe all of the islands in this group, and the bright yellow finches that flitted about the arid slopes were then named after the islands they inhabited.

The Islands are also known for their many microsystems. Hot, dry air from the Sahara converges with cool, moist air from the ocean to create seventy distinct ecological communities. The islands have broad-leaf evergreen forests, palm groves, pine forests, and high mountain vegetation, as well as deserts. Their laurisilva forests are living fossils, remnants of ancient trees that covered much of the planet 20 million years ago.

Relative isolation has given rise to a great number of creatures unique to the Canaries. With little interference from the mainland, birds, reptiles, plants, and mammals quickly evolve to adapt to their environment. Charles Darwin called the islands "perhaps one of the most interesting places in the world" in the diary he kept during his voyage on *The Beagle*. (Unfortunately, he was unable to explore the islands due to a cholera quarantine.) The Canary Islands have thousands of endemic species—animals and plants that do not naturally live anywhere else—and every six days a new species is found. The island of Tenerife has the highest concentration of endemic species in Europe.

Many of these endemic species are rare and critically endangered. Fewer than 400 El Hierro giant lizards remain. The sixty-centimetre dark grey or brown lizard with orange spotting was thought to have been hunted to extinction in the 1930s—first by humans for its delicious taste and then by introduced rats, cats, and dogs—until a small population was rediscovered in 1974. The blue chaffinch, a type of finch, is listed as near threatened; a subspecies that lives only on Gran Canaria has dwindled to fewer than 250. These birds are quite picky about where they live—only in pine forests at seven hundred to two thousand metres above sea level—and much of their habitat has been destroyed by logging and forest fires.

The importance of conservation to islanders has soared. One of the biggest issues the Canary Islands face is the introduction of invasive species. According to government officials, a foreign species crosses their borders every seventeen days, and twice a year that invader grows to severely threaten indigenous plants and animals.

There would be no risk of us introducing foreign invaders to the Canary Islands: we would relish their beauty from afar. As the sun moved across the sky, I watched the changing hues of the reddish-brown slopes and scanned the waters for fishing or pleasure boats out for a day excursion. We were still too far from land to make out any communities, but we expected to see their lights after sunset.

Due to the spread of the Canary Islands and our slow passage, we remained in the vicinity for several days. We found the continual sight of land in the distance comforting. The winds remained calm, so we didn't fear being driven into the distant cliffs.

On our third day among the islands, I sat perched on the gunwale, washing tapioca bits from the breakfast pot. Suddenly four trout-sized fish zipped around, sucking up the pieces of tapioca that drifted to the ocean floor. Colin joined me, and we watched the grey and black striped fish dart back and forth. We scraped pudding off the unwashed plates and held the creamy bits in the water. The fish nibbled the food fearlessly right from our hands. Colin reached his hand into the water and stroked the back of a fish while he continued to feed it with his other hand.

"I think we might have pets. Perhaps if we feed them regularly, they'll stay with us," Colin said, beaming.

"I'm naming this guy, here, Ned," I said, pointing to the smallest fish of the group. "He looks like a Ned."

"Okay, well, this fish with the scar on his back is Fred, then, and the guy with the chunk out of his tail can be Ted," Colin volunteered.

The fish wriggled enthusiastically to keep up with our drifting boat.

"Ned, Ted, and Fred," I said. "That sounds good. How about the fourth guy?"

"Dead?" Colin said.

"No, with a name like that he'll be the first to be eaten by a shark. How about Oscar?"

"Sure," said Colin. "Do you know what kind of fish these are?"

I pulled out our fish identification guide, and we learned that our new friends were pilot fish. I wondered how they came by their name, and whether it had anything to do with them "piloting" boats across the sea. Even if they didn't have any ideas about the course we should take, it felt wonderful having them at our side—like having company after you've been alone for too long.

It wasn't unusual for pilot fish to travel with company. In fact, they survive by following larger creatures, such as sharks, sea turtles, and rays, and dining on any leftover scraps from their prey, as well as on surface parasites. Sharks are extremely tolerant of pilot fish, even allowing them into their open mouths to pick scraps from between their teeth. We later learned that pilot fish loyally follow boats across oceans, perhaps in a case of mistaken identity. If the fish decided to follow our boat, we would make sure to reward them for their efforts. Just like a larger animal, we left a trail of edible leftovers and had enough barnacles growing on our hull to feed a pilot fish army.

The one thing we couldn't provide to the pilot fish— something that comes with their symbiotic relationship with sharks—was protection. Predators generally stay away from the pilot fish while they swim beside sharks. We could only hope that Ned, Ted, Fred, and Oscar would be able to fend for themselves.

We were not the only ones fascinated by this fish. In his poem "The Maldive Shark," published in 1888, Herman Melville wrote of the "sleek little pilot-fish, azure and slim," describing how they found safety in the shark's mouth:

They have nothing of harm to dread,
But liquidly glide on his ghastly flank
Or before his Gorgonian head;
Or lurk in the port of serrated teeth
In white triple tiers of glittering gates,
And there find a haven when peril's abroad,
An asylum in jaws of the Fates!

In the days that followed, we learned to expect the splashings of our new quartet at lunch and dinner, when bits of leftovers went overboard and into their eager mouths. I crooned sweet nothings to our new friends as they bodychecked each other in enthusiastic attacks on my plate. Our companions brought excitement and a new topic of conversation to the boat. We fussed over them as if they were a litter of kittens we'd just adopted. When we rowed, moving at two to three knots, they would tirelessly swim after us, wagging their little tails to keep up. Unlike Colin and I, who received a break from the oars every two hours, our fish friends had few breaks from the toil.

OCTOBER 22 MARKED the first day of our second month at sea. We were at just over twenty-eight degrees latitude, or about five hundred kilometres north of the tropics. A hot sun blazed from a cloudless sky, and I was sweating profusely as I pulled the oars. At the end of one of my shifts, I lowered the bucket over the side, scooping up several gallons of cool seawater. As Colin mumbled and bumbled his way out of the cabin, I poured the refreshing liquid over my head. Then, as I dipped the bucket back in for a few seconds, I noticed something flashing in the depths.

"There's something big down below!" I yelled.

By now, Colin had made his way out of the cabin, and he stood beside me, peering down. A metre-long fish was emerging from the depths.

"That's not big," Colin said. "I thought you meant a shark or something."

"He's big enough to eat Ned, Ted, and crew," I said nervously, as the sleek fish approached our hull.

"Hey, that's a dorado. I used to eat those all the time in the Pacific. They're great eating," Colin exclaimed.

I grabbed the fishing rod, which conveniently had a rubber squid attached to the hook. I was motivated by both a hunger for fresh meat and a desire to protect our piscine pets from this marauding predator. As soon as the green rubber squid hit the water, the dorado dashed towards the lure, and its yellow colouring changed slightly to a less noticeable blue/grey. At the last second, it veered away.

The dorado had a bulbous head with a long, tapered body. As I moved the lure back and forth across the water by moving the tip of the rod in sweeping arcs, the sleek fish dashed after it. It moved with incredible speed, and I wasn't surprised to later find out that dorado—also known as dolphin fish and mahi-mahi—are even faster than some sharks, reaching speeds of ninety kilometres per hour.

After about four or five strikes, the rod jerked and the tip bent towards the water. The line began screaming out as the fish tried to make an escape. Eventually, after much leaping, the fish began to tire, and I was able to reel it in slowly.

As the exhausted fish neared the boat, I noticed Ned and crew emerge from the depths, and they approached with curiosity. Colin used a gaff to haul the dorado on board.

"Well done," I said, in awe.

But our dinner was not yet guaranteed. The fish had slipped off the hook and was now careening around the deck, propelling itself by frantically flopping. If it got lucky, it might find an escape route down one of the scuppers, but we weren't about to let that happen. I ran after it, trying to end its misery with a hit from the blunt end of the gaff. But I seemed to hit the deck more often than the fish and, by the time it was over, our boat looked like a slaughterhouse.

The dorado is beautiful, even in death. In the water, it shimmers bright gold with blue and green hues. But its colours are always changing, dimming, and brightening to facilitate hunting and communication. In death it runs through a palette of hues—silver, blue, gold, green, and brown—before becoming a final muted yellow.

I felt a pang of remorse at ending its life. Although the fish we'd just caught was swimming alone, dorados mate for life. Most likely, I'd made a fish out there terribly lonely. But I consoled myself with the fact that the U.K.'s Marine Conservation Society considers dorado to be one of the more sustainable fish (when caught by hand lining methods in small fisheries) because of their rapid development and short lifespan. It takes the fish three to four years to grow from eggs drifting in sargassum—a type of seaweed that grows mid-ocean—into thirty-pound adults.

"Do we have any lemons left?" Colin asked eagerly. "We could pan-fry him in olive oil with a little lemon squeezed on top and then have rice and maybe some vegetables on the side."

I had never cooked a whole fish before and wasn't exactly sure where to begin. How did the seafood counter transform this huge chunk of skin, bones, and guts into tidy fillets?

"I'll clean and fillet the fish," Colin offered.

"I'll cook it, then," I said with relief.

Colin used the sharp blade from our Gerber multi-tool to make a long slit along the belly, from the base of the head to the tail. He deftly reached in with his hand, pulled out the innards, and showed them to me.

"You can see what he's been eating," Colin said as he pointed to a tiny fish. "It's a flying fish. They glide through the air using their fins. I used to see them all the time on my sailboat when I was on the Pacific, but I wasn't sure if we'd see them here."

The flying fish had not yet been digested, so I could clearly make out its features. It was small and unremarkable, except for its fins, which were enormous for its tiny size and spread out like an unfurled paper fan. They looked like wings.

Colin continued filleting the dorado. He made a longitudinal cut along the backbone to remove the first fillet, then flipped the fish over, and with a single cut he removed the remainder of the fish from the skeleton. He proudly handed the two fillets to me.

"You've done that before, haven't you?" I said, admiring his work.

Fortunately, Colin had learned to fillet fish when he worked on a salmon troller. He'd perfected his technique in the five years he had spent sailing.

We placed the fillets into our aluminum pot and hid the pot away in a cool, shady corner. We washed the deck with seawater and threw the remains to our pilot fish. They frantically darted back and forth, trying to claim their dinner before gravity did. It was a happy day for all the fish, except one.

With only one single-burner stove, cooking a two-pot meal is challenging. I prepared the rice, removed the pot from the burner when it was two-thirds cooked, and wrapped it in a blanket to hold in the heat. Then I dipped the fish fillets in flour spiced with garlic powder, pepper, and salt, and dropped them into the hot frying pan. A rich aroma of frying fish and garlic permeated the air. When both sides were crisp and brown, I lay the fish on a bed of fluffy rice with cold chopped tomatoes and black olives from a can on the side. Then I drizzled lemon juice over everything.

"Dinner's almost ready," I said.

Colin quickly stowed the oars and wriggled his feet out of the rowing shoes. Dinnertime was always highly anticipated—we stopped rowing and ate our meal together—but never as much as tonight.

Colin clambered from the rowing platform and made a cushioned seat by placing a life jacket against the safety line. I stayed in the cabin, leaning out the open hatch.

"This is amazing. It looks like something you could serve at Thanksgiving," Colin said as I passed him his yellow plastic plate piled high with food.

"Do you know what 'dorado' means in Spanish?" I asked.

"What?"

"Gold."

Colin bit into one of the crispy chunks. It was cooked to perfection, and the flesh was tender yet firm.

"I see why," Colin said, nodding his head slowly.

Their name seemed just as appropriate as that of the pilot fish who continued to swim with us. Though some know dorado as mahi-mahi, which means "strong strong" in Hawaiian, we always called them dorado.

With the occasional contented murmur, we finished the entire six-pound fish. In one meal, we had consumed more protein than we normally did in a week. Our overworked muscles would be grateful.

Although our regular meals were healthy and balanced, they were lower in protein than they should have been. This seemed to be reflected in the way our bodies responded to the strenuous exercise. I had thought that ten hours of rowing would add considerable muscle mass, but my muscles weren't bulging and I still had enough fat to cushion me on the rowing seat. Perhaps our workout was akin to that of a long-distance runner. Few who win marathons resemble Schwarzenegger. Still, I hoped our added protein would help me gain *some* muscle.

THE FOLLOWING DAY we were treated to favourable twenty-kilometre-an-hour winds from the northeast. Our boat slipped through the water at 3.2 knots and Ned, Ted, Fred, and Oscar wriggled vigorously to keep up. As our boat's speed increased, they began swimming farther out along the flanks of our vessel. Eventually they swam right in the region where the oars dipped into the water. More than once I felt a little *thunk* as a fish took a paddle to the face.

I pulled long, easy strokes on the oars, and a small trail of bubbles followed our boat. Ahead I could just make out the smudge of Tenerife, the best-known island in the Canaries. Colin poked his head through the roof hatch in the cabin and observed the sea.

"Do you see that?" Colin said, looking dead astern.

I couldn't see anything. "What?"

"It's either a big fish or a dolphin," Colin said.

An abrupt splashing erupted around the boat, and six or seven dolphins appeared. It was hard to tell if they were just playing around or if they were hunting. The scent of fishy breath filled the air.

Suddenly I was gripped by dread.

"Where are our fish?" I cried.

Colin was silent as he surveyed the cavorting dolphins. I stopped rowing and peered over the side. I could see nothing but a limitless chasm of blue and the occasional rocketing dolphin.

"Ned ... Ted?" I called hopefully.

The dolphins vanished as quickly as they came, and our pets were nowhere to be seen. I tossed a bit of dorado meat into the water, a treat I had been planning to feed our fish at lunch. I waited, expecting them to dash out of the shadows, to peck voraciously at the food. Usually Oscar would be out first, followed shortly after by the others.

Nothing.

I watched the white piece of meat slowly spin out of sight on its way to the bottom of the ocean. Ned, Ted, Fred, and Oscar were gone.

In terms of rowing, we were making good progress, but I was despondent and sulky. The loss of our friends made our solitude more pronounced. We had failed to protect them. Evolution had honed the instinct that mistakenly drew them to us in search of food and protection, but we had not provided the latter. I felt guilty that we had been unable to help our naive little fish.

All day I peered into the blue waters, hoping to catch a glimpse of the quartet. But I didn't see a thing.

TENERIFE IS THE largest of the Canary Islands and we had spotted it from more than a hundred kilometres away, but it took us two more days to discern the features of the landscape. Like Kilimanjaro, Tenerife's massive peak, Teide, is a freestanding mountain created from a volcanic eruption. It is the world's third-largest volcano; the last eruption took place in 1909. The eastern side of the island had steep brown slopes and folded valleys. We saw no snow on top of the mountain, but it does receive occasional dustings. We knew that once we passed Tenerife, we wouldn't see land again for several months on the other side of the Atlantic Ocean.

Although we continued in almost perfect conditions, I didn't feel entirely happy. The disappointment at not being rejoined by our finned friends lingered. I missed dangling my hands over the side and having them nibbling on my fingers. And these feelings of sadness fuelled a growing dissatisfaction with our monotonous world. I stopped admiring the colours that played on the ocean's surface at sunrise and the beauty of shearwaters that soared effortlessly in the overhead breezes. I no longer relished the feeling of well-worked muscles at day's end or the refreshing sensation of diving into warm ocean waters. I was in a downward spiral that dredged forth my doubts and insecurities.

What was I doing here? Had I given up a world I was comfortable in and a career that I had worked hard to achieve for a trivial pursuit? I had spent seven years completing my undergraduate and graduate studies and several more interning and working entry-level positions before finally establishing a solid career, only to discover it wasn't nearly as fulfilling as I had imagined. I clearly remember the words of a long-term boyfriend as our relationship began to fade: "You'll never be happy with what you have. You always want change." Maybe that was true. Moving has always been a part of my life. I've lived in numerous cities, never in one place for more than four years. Since my first job—a paper route at the age of twelve—I've had more than a dozen jobs and a career that's gone from research and teaching to business development.

I wasn't entirely sure if my rowing odyssey was a fork in the road, or just a break from the path I was already on. I felt uncomfortable with the notion of abandoning my years of education, so it was easier to think of this trip as a long pause in my career—a chance to embark on a different kind of challenge. Unlike many of my peers, I had never taken a year off to go backpacking in Europe or Australia. I had always stared ahead with tunnel vision as I moved towards my distant career. Perhaps a year on the road (and on the water) would be a healthy change.

I grew up with the ingrained notion that life is meant to be hard work, not a pursuit of pleasures. Both my parents are immigrants who came to Canada to provide a better life for their children, and I was their only child. It was my obligation to take advantage of this land of opportunity.

My parents did not lead only through words; their lives exemplified hard work. My father had left Syria for Canada with only a pocketful of change. He worked nights as a waiter and days as a security guard, and somehow managed to get a university degree at the same time. He met my mother, a German immigrant, during his first year here. My mother's life was also difficult. When she was seven months old, her mother died; she lost her father in the Soviet Union's Gulag camps of World War II. Her family lived in East Prussia, but during World War II the country was ravaged and eventually divided between the Soviet Union and Poland. At the age of eleven, my mother, her aunt, and two cousins successfully escaped East Prussia on their third attempt; over five difficult months in the winter of 1946, they travelled illegally and without money by foot and train, living in refugee camps and carrying all their meagre belongings on their backs, eventually reaching West Germany. In her early thirties, my mother immigrated to North America with her cousin in search of a better life.

Since I was young, I have noticed differences in the philosophies between new immigrants such as my parents and multi-generation Canadians who have always lived in a society free of war and starvation. The struggles my parents faced left them with survivalist attitudes and an outlook that emphasizes financial well-being. They don't let their emotions show or talk about their fears or weaknesses. I was brought up in two worlds: one where being open about one's emotions was encouraged, and the other where this was regarded as a weakness.

Whether I would go to university was never questioned— this was the only route to financial prosperity. I had little money to put towards my education, but I drew on loans, grants, and scholarships to supplement earnings from summer jobs. Before the ink dried on my Master's dissertation, I had several jobs to choose from. When I decided I wanted to use my biotechnology education to develop therapeutics through business instead of research, I found individuals who were more than willing to mentor me. These opportunities were not available to my parents—or, for that matter, to 80 per cent of the world's population living in less prosperous countries—and having them profoundly altered my view of life. Although a career was no less important to me than it was to my parents, a job that offered opportunities to learn and be challenged began to take priority over one with financial stability.

But now, as we bobbed on the open ocean, still seven thousand kilometres from our destination, I couldn't help but wonder if I'd made the right choice. We would arrive home more than fifty thousand dollars in debt. I would have no job, and would face the struggle of getting back into the work force. The way things looked, we might both be facing personal bankruptcy. These financial troubles gnawed at me while I laboured at the oars. The world of banks and credit cards and creditors seemed another planet away, but we couldn't forget about them.

Colin listened as I aired my worries and, as usual, helped to put things in perspective.

"You'll never starve in Canada, and you'll always have a roof over your head, which is much more than what many people in the world have," he said. "It's too easy to allow external pressures to dictate what we strive for, and not what really makes us happy. This row across the Atlantic Ocean will create memories that you will take to your grave. The dolphins, the sharks, the storms, the struggles—it's all price-less. Your years of work will all blur into one another. But this year won't. Believe me, forty years down the road, you're not going to kick yourself for having rowed across an ocean."

I nodded in full agreement. I knew all that, but somehow I couldn't shift thirty years of conditioning so easily.

"No matter what happens, we'll have each other," Colin added.

It was sweet and corny and true all at the same time. It reminded me of the Tom Waits song "House Where Nobody Lives." The lyrics "If there's love in the house..." went through my head, and I couldn't help but smile. At least we had a seven-metre palace.

TWO DAYS LATER we found ourselves in the middle of the 120-kilometre passage between Gran Canaria and Fuerte-ventura. A microclimate in the region, created by the uneven heating of the land and ocean, affected both the weather and wind direction. The winds shifted early in the day, and we now had headwinds from the south, decreasing our progress to that of a slow walk. The wildlife continued to entertain; we saw a small pod of dolphins and a mid-sized shark in addi-tion to the dorado, tuna, petrels, and shearwaters that we now saw on a daily basis. But the wildlife was not the only thing that multiplied; we also saw numerous boats, both local fish-ing trawlers and freighters, transporting goods to the islands. The memory of our near collision with the tanker was all too vivid, and I felt apprehensive as the waters became increas-ingly congested.

Before heading off to bed, I noticed that a thick cloud cover obscured the stars, but that numerous lights shone from non-celestial sources. Off in the distance, the city lights of Las Palmas de Gran Canaria emitted more illumination than a full moon. Several other towns and villages on the islands gave off muted yellowish glows that reflected on the clouds above. And at any given time, we could see between five and ten green or red lights, the running lights of nearby boats.

By law, powered boats on the water must display running lights at night, which announce both their presence and direction of heading. A green light shines from the starboard side, red off the port, and white off the stern. Knowing this, boats can determine one another's orientations and approximate heading. For example, if we saw a green light, we knew that we were seeing the right side of a ship and that its direction of movement would be rightward. If we saw both red and green lights together, we knew that the ship was coming directly towards us. Upon departing Lisbon, we had had this unsettling experience a few times, but invariably the vessel would change course when it saw our own navigation light. Colin had cynically dubbed this disturbing display of green and red lights "a Christmas treat."

Because of our boat's slow speed and its erratic movement in big waves, we displayed a bright flashing strobe light instead of the typical red, green, and white display. So far this had been very effective in alerting nearby boats of our presence at night.

At 1:50 AM Colin woke me from a deep sleep. He was outside rowing and I could hear him talking loudly, probably to some dolphins splashing around the boat. I couldn't help feeling annoyed that he was interrupting my precious few hours of sleep. Trying to ignore him, I slid my head under the pillow.

"We've got a Christmas treat," he said.

My bed was warm and cozy. I was still groggy with sleep and certainly not ready for the bow of a ship to come crashing through the wall. I quickly threw on a shirt and opened the hatch.

"Where is it?"

"Straight over there," Colin said, pointing off the starboard side.

I could clearly see the bright green and red lights.

"It's been coming at us for a while. It's a calm, clear night. I've got no idea why they can't see our strobe light," Colin said.

"Maybe it's our strobe that's attracting them," I said nervously. "I'll try calling them on the VHF."

I dug out the VHF radio and a package of signalling flares. Colin propelled the rowboat with all his might in an attempt to move us out of the ship's path.

"This is *Ondine*, a small rowing vessel displaying a strobe light; we are calling an unidentified vessel bearing straight for us. Do you copy?" I said into the VHF.

I waited for an answer. Silence. I checked the radio to make sure it was functioning and on channel sixteen. The LED function light shone brightly. I tried again but with more urgency in my voice. Nothing.

Colin had turned the boat several degrees and was rowing a course perpendicular to the lights. Our speed was almost four knots, and *Ondine* cut smoothly through the flat waters. It soon became apparent that the other ship was changing course to keep coming towards us. The navigation lights were now very bright, and we could also hear the rumble of a diesel engine. We doubted it was an official vessel. If

it was, both the coast guard and the police would be monitoring the radio.

It was impossible to gauge the distance of the vessel until
the hull suddenly became discernable one or two hundred
metres away. We were terrified. In moments, it would slam
into us.

"STOP! YOU'RE GOING TO RUN US OVER!" I screamed
into the radio.

I ripped the flare out of the pouch. The ship was so close.
I could see the form of the boat illuminated by the pulses
of our strobe. It was a wooden fishboat, about twenty-four
metres long, with a high wheelhouse. Something was wrong.
The flare wouldn't go off.

"I can't light it!" I screamed.

The wooden fishboat was now twenty-five metres from us,
moving at full cruising speed. Impact would be in seconds.
Colin was in the midst of a turn, trying to avoid the impend-
ing collision. Our carbon-fibre oars looked like they were
going to snap under the stress.

Suddenly the fishing vessel turned sharply. They were
taking evasive action. It seemed too late, and I braced for
the impact. But the vessel missed us by less than two metres.
Colin tucked the starboard oar against our boat to avoid having it sheared off. A wave rocked our vessel violently, and
then the fishboat continued full speed into the distance, the
rumble of its engine slowly fading to silence.

Colin dropped his oars in relief and exhaustion. He was
panting heavily.

"That was too close," he gasped. "There was a glow inside
the wheelhouse—probably from the instrument panels. I
could see two guys peering through the window. The fellow

who saw us first wasn't the one at the helm. He grabbed the wheel out of the helmsman's hands and cranked it hard."

My heart kept racing as I watched the boat's white stern light fading into the distance. I wondered if they would have stopped if they'd run us over.

"They may have thought our strobe was marking something of interest, maybe fishing nets," Colin said. "A strobe doesn't allow for any depth perception, so they wouldn't have known how far away we were. They probably figured the light was still miles away."

Several boats were still in sight, and we worried about another incident. We pondered turning off the strobe, but instead kept a vigilant watch. The night passed without further incident.

9

THE GREAT WHITE
SHARK

Any floating object on the ocean quickly collects a thick mat of barnacles, seaweed, and algae. Our boat was no exception, and the growth on our hull was significantly decreasing our speed. The antifouling paint we had applied in Lisbon was doing very little to prevent barnacle buildup.

One day Colin decided to jump overboard to scrub the hull. Armed with a snorkel, mask, and bristle brush, he scraped away five weeks of crustacean growth and algal slime. I peered into the water, watching dislodged crustaceans plummet into the blue abyss and the occasional fish dart after the sinking loot. My job was to scan for sharks and to alert Colin if I saw one. We knew the likelihood of an attack was low but felt it was best to be prudent. After all, our chance of being hit by a hurricane had been statistically less likely than being eaten by a shark, too.

After an hour and a half, Colin finished scraping and clambered back into the boat. "She's cleaner than a nun's bum," he said.

I rolled my eyes at his analogy, and Colin's grin broadened.

"No wonder we were going so slowly. Some of those barnacles were four inches long."

I climbed back onto the rowing seat and put Colin's efforts to the test. It took a few minutes to overcome inertia and bring the boat to cruising speed. We were travelling at 1.5 knots, just under three kilometres an hour, which was pretty good considering we still had stiff headwinds.

"Awesome work, Tiger," I said. "We're moving much faster."

"We'll have to do this every week."

It was amazing how quickly the barnacles had formed on the bottom of our boat. I had read earlier that they float on the ocean currents in their larval stage until they find a suitable home. Then they attach themselves, metamorphose into small shellfish, and stay put for the rest of their lives. Each barnacle builds a shell and reaches out with a series of sieve-like fingers that strain plankton from the seawater. As I watched them feed, I thought of a cluster of fiddlehead ferns unfurling themselves with tiny feathery arms instead of leaves.

Although barnacles are a well-known headache for boaters, humans are a greater threat to them—and not just to those that make their home on the boat hulls. Because the ocean is becoming more acidic, barnacles' shells are getting weaker and weaker. The increased acidity of the ocean is a threat not only to barnacles, but to oysters, snails, coral reefs, starfish, sea urchins, shrimp, certain types of plankton, and all ocean organisms that build a calcium carbonate shell or skeleton. In fact, a third of all marine life is in peril.

According to U.S. scientist Scott C. Doney, the acidity of the ocean has increased 30 per cent since the industrial revolution began because of increased carbon dioxide levels in the atmosphere. The oceans have absorbed half the carbon dioxide emissions, dampening the impact of climate change at a great cost. When carbon dioxide dissolves in the ocean, it becomes carbonic acid and causes the ocean's pH to drop. Usually the ocean is kept in balance by marine organisms, which convert the dissolved carbon dioxide products into calcium carbonate skeletons or shells. When carbon dioxide levels are slightly higher, these creatures become more prolific. But now that humans emit 27 billion tonnes of CO_2 a year, the oceans simply cannot keep up.

All marine animals that build their skeletons or shells with calcium carbonate ($CaCO_3$) need to create it from building materials in the ocean—namely calcium and carbonate ions. (They cannot use existing $CaCO_3$ deposits to build their structures.) But carbonate ions, which are naturally found at supersaturated levels, are dwindling as oceans absorb more carbon dioxide. Like brick-layers running low on bricks, crustaceans have a more difficult time building a structure. By 2050, some areas of the ocean will have too little carbonate for animals to create shells. And with increasing acidity, animals will struggle to build their chalky skeletons and shells; like pearls in vinegar, their calcium carbonate structures will dissolve.

This is bad news for the people who rely on the ocean for survival, too. The last time the ocean reached such acidic levels may have been when dinosaurs became extinct. Sixty-five million years ago, the dinosaurs were killed off by what most experts believe was an enormous meteorite or a comet that slammed into the Yucatán Peninsula, a portion of Mexico where the earth has high concentrations of calcium sulphate. The heat and pressure created by the impact caused the calcium sulphate to convert into sulphuric compounds, which reacted with oxygen and water to form sulphuric acid. If as little as 5 per cent of these sulphuric compounds rained down into the oceans, the environment created would have been lethally corrosive. When the dinosaurs died, almost all marine animals that created calcium carbonate shells or skeletons also disappeared. Most species of calcium carbonate-shelled plankton disappeared, as did mussels. Coral reefs vanished and did not reappear for at least two million years.

According to research by the Carnegie Institution of Washington's Dr. Ken Caldeira, if rising carbon dioxide levels continue unabated, oceans may face a mass extinction similar to that which occurred when dinosaurs disappeared. When Dr. Caldeira presented his findings at the AGU/ASLO Ocean Sciences Meeting in Honolulu in 2006, they created headlines around the world. If a similar mass extinction should happen, recovery will not be easy. The geologic record demonstrates that the chemical effects of ocean acidification would last tens of thousands of years, and the recovery of species would take millions.

But for now at least, the barnacles in our neck of the woods seemed to be doing just fine. Their biggest worry was a guy in a snorkelling mask with a bristle brush.

AFTER MY ROWING shift, I relaxed in the cabin and fixed myself a lunch of brochette, cheese, and crackers. I washed it all down with some black tea that Colin had left simmering in a pot. I was just about to start writing in my journal when Colin called for me to come out and see some dolphins.

"I'll be out in a minute," I said. Dolphins were becoming a regular occurrence.

"There's a whale, too," Colin added.

That sounded exciting. I emerged from the cabin with our large video camera. But I was already too late; the dolphins were swimming away, and the whale was submerged.

"What's that?" Colin said, as he pointed to a small, dark dorsal fin about ten metres away. At first I thought it could be the whale or a large dolphin. But the fin did not rise to reveal the curve of a dolphin's back or move in the slow manner that typified other visiting whales. Instead, it sliced through the water, a black blade cutting a straight line through the surface of the sea. I was mesmerized at what was undoubtedly our best shark sighting so far.

But the fin was more like the tip of the iceberg. The shark's behemoth bulk was hidden beneath the water. When the shark rose to the water's surface, the dark triangle quadrupled in size.

"Oh my God, that looks like the sail on a windsurfer," Colin said.

The fin had risen to tower more than a metre. Its enormous appendage created a small V of ripples as it cut through the water. This could only be a great white shark, the only shark in these waters that can reach that size.

To coincide with my quickening heart rate, the shark's pace sped up. Normally, great whites cruise at a leisurely pace but they quickly increase velocity during an attack to

reach speeds of forty kilometres an hour. They can even gen-
erate enough speed to launch their two-thousand-kilogram-
plus bodies completely out of the water.

Why was this shark accelerating? I couldn't help but feel
concerned, and I knew my gut reaction was worth taking
seriously. A perusal of statistics compiled by the International
Shark Attack File shows that great white sharks have attacked
and sunk boats ranging from sea kayaks to sailboats and have
knocked people overboard.

We stared in awe as the shark circled our boat a second time. Colin added the soundtrack of the two-note *Jaws*
theme song:

"Dun, dun, dun-dun, dun-dun, dun-dun."

The fin eventually disappeared, and the sea seemed empty
once again. But as if watching a horror movie in which the
antagonist leaves the screen, we waited apprehensively for a
sudden reappearance. The shark could be less than a stone's
throw away, completely invisible beneath the surface.

"Fancy going for a swim?" Colin asked.

"Thank God that Jaws didn't visit us a few hours earlier,
when you were scraping the bottom of the boat," I said.

"You might have been rowing to Florida alone."

"Don't joke about that," I said, still nervous that the shark
might be around.

I had read Sylvia Cook and John Fairfax's book, *Oars
Across the Pacific*, detailing their 361-day row across the
Pacific Ocean. Fairfax was a risk-taking, womanizing gam-
bler who liked to fight sharks to raise money for his rowing
expeditions. When he was rowing across the Pacific Ocean,
he continued to embrace his penchant for danger and had

his arm sliced through to the bone by a three-metre shark. Sylvia had sewn up his wounds and rowed the remaining thousand kilometres to land where he could see a doctor.

"I bet removing those barnacles was a calling card for carnivores," Colin said. "I watched all those mashed, meaty bodies rain down into the depths. It must have smelled like a doughnut shop for sharks."

"Maybe we shouldn't scrape the hull anymore," I said. Next it would be my turn, and I didn't relish the prospect.

Colin ignored my comment and pointed to the waters twenty metres in front of us. "The whale is back."

I could see the large dark grey form slowly approach our boat, and I moved the video camera towards it. It began its slide directly beneath our boat, about a metre beneath the surface. The animal's girth was as large as the beam of our boat; it looked to be at least six metres long. I was amazed to see such a majestic creature just inches from our hull, moving with the gentle care that I had come to expect of whales. I wanted to reach down and touch its back.

Through the viewfinder of the video camera, I noticed something seemed odd about the whale's tail. It was aligned vertically to its body, not horizontally. I glanced up from the LCD display for a clearer view. This tail was just like the dorado we had caught, but about a thousand times bigger.

"That's the shark," I said in a low voice.

I don't think I've ever been so mesmerized—or perhaps frozen with fear might be a more accurate description. Just an arm's length away swam a hulking two-thousand-kilogram carnivore looking for lunch. It eyed the hull of our boat, wondering if we would make a good meal, trying to decide whether to take a test bite.

This is how great white sharks attack humans. It's not that the shark particularly enjoys *Homo sapiens*—we're rather bony and muscled and lacking in fat, compared with sea mammals. But they don't know this until they take a test bite. Apparently it's more like a gentle nibble, and I've even heard some call it "mouthing"—as when a puppy puts its mouth around your arm without biting hard. Unfortunately, even a nibble from the greatest predator in the sea can have lethal consequences. After the initial bite of human flesh, most sharks don't come back for seconds, but the damage may have already been done.

With our quarter-inch plywood hull, even an affectionate lick from our new friend would probably send the boat to the bottom—leaving Colin and I as morsels for dessert.

The shark finished its slow slide under our boat and vanished from view.

"Wow," I said, exhaling.

"I thought we were goners," Colin said, half-seriously.

"That's not out of the question yet."

We both stared into the water looking for shadows or dorsal fins. After five minutes, Colin said, "Looks like the coast is clear. Maybe we should get back to rowing."

I was mildly disappointed. The shark frightened me and aroused my curiosity at the same time. After all, seeing a great white shark is a once-in-a-lifetime experience, and the biologist in me wanted a chance to examine it in greater detail.

"If only our boat was a little more solid, we could throw some food overboard to lure him back."

Colin stared at me for a second before bursting into laughter.

"What? I'm sure any marine biologist would be excited to have the opportunity to observe a shark that large," I said.

The shark didn't come back, so we relived the event through the video camera. We huddled in the cabin and rewound the tape. I had not caught the shark circling the boat, but the camera had been rolling when it passed underneath. Since we didn't have a polarizing filter, glare blocked most of the details, but the shark's gargantuan size was displayed clearly.

"That is by far the largest shark I've ever seen," Colin said. "He's as big as our boat."

I felt quite privileged to have seen such a large shark on my first ocean crossing. Based on Colin's experiences and the accounts of other sailors, I knew it was uncommon to see a great white unless one travels to areas they are known to frequent, such as the waters off South Africa.

The shark that visited us was significantly larger than average. When we played the video footage frame by frame, we guessed the shark was over seven metres. Even if we over-measured by a metre, it was still substantial. Shark scientists estimate that the maximum size for the great white is between six and seven and a half metres, although five and a half metres is considered a giant.

Colin went back to rowing, and I flipped through the pages of our SAS Survival Guide to see what they had to say about sharks.

"It says here that a good swimmer can outmanoeuvre a shark," I said, laughing.

"You've got to be kidding me."

"Not at all. It says you can escape an attacking shark by making sharp turns."

"I'd like to see the author try that," Colin said.

A great white can swim five times faster than an Olympic swimmer and they hunt some of the fastest and most agile marine creatures, including dolphins, tuna, and dorado. Not only can they reach speeds in excess of forty kilometres an hour, but they can turn on a dime. I couldn't imagine any human swimmer capable of zigzagging out of the way of a refrigerator-sized mouth charging forward at the speed of a car. Over time, sharks had to evolve into capable hunters; otherwise they would not have survived 450 million years of natural selection. They even survived the catastrophe that extinguished the dinosaurs and 95 per cent of all marine life.

Everything from their colour and sophisticated sensory system to their power of thermoregulation has been honed to perfection by the force of evolution. Sharks are two-toned, white on the bottom and grey on top, so that they blend into the brightness of the sky from below, and into the darkness of the ocean depths from above. Even when seen from the side, their colour division breaks up their outline. Unlike most fish, they are not completely cold-blooded; a complex circulatory system allows blood in certain vital regions to be warmer than the surrounding water temperatures, allowing them to move and react more quickly. They also have a sixth sense—as if sight, sound, touch, taste, and smell weren't enough—allowing them to detect electromagnetic impulses at the unimaginably low level of half a billionth of a volt. In other words, they can sense the nervous system of any living creatures nearby. We had been running our solar-powered desalinator earlier, and I wondered if that electrical generation may have also attracted the shark.

Like pretty much everyone who watched Steven Spielberg's movie *Jaws*, I am terrified by the great white's powerful jaws and teeth. Unlike most animals, which possess only two rows of teeth, sharks have six—two on the top and four on the bottom. The extra rows come out at different stages of growth, some visible and others just beneath the surface, so that every six to eight weeks, a row is replaced. At any given time, a great white has about four hundred teeth in its mouth and uses eighty of those for biting. Each individual tooth is shaped like a miniature saw, serrated edges cutting through meat and bone as the shark shakes its head back and forth.

But not all the features that allowed sharks to flourish for hundreds of millions of years serve them well now. Slow maturation and a low birthrate limit the ability of shark populations to rebound from decreases they've faced from fishing and purposeful slaughter. In 2003 Canadian scientist Julia Baum published a study in the prestigious journal *Science* showing that the great white shark population in the North Atlantic had dropped 79 per cent since 1986. Since then there has been no sign of the population rebounding. Recovery will be difficult, if not impossible. Yet for the most part, sharks get little sympathy and fewer conservation campaigns than arguably cuter, or at least less toothy, species. Is it fear that prevents us from showing them comparable compassion? Perhaps. But what an impressive creature.

A STRONG CURRENT funnelled between the islands of Fuerteventura and Gran Canaria, propelling us forward. We could see the volcanic mountains rising from the sea during the day and the glittering city lights at night. After five weeks at sea, the allure of land was powerful. Promises of freshly brewed coffee, fruits, salads, and cold drinks lay just a few kilometres away. Even beyond these cravings, we had practical reasons for going ashore. We'd lost both our sea anchors and could probably find a replacement here. We could also replenish our food supply in case the journey ahead took longer than anticipated. But the risk of being blown into the rocks as we neared the harbour was too high. We also knew that, if we needed to, we could stretch our food supply by rationing. And, for the moment, our makeshift drogue seemed to be working just fine.

Although I knew our decision was the prudent choice, I felt a pang of anxiety as we pointed our bow towards the open ocean and away from the Canary Islands. It would be at least five thousand kilometres and many months before we saw land again, and there was no turning back. The aft winds and currents increased as we continued rowing west to the other side of the ocean.

AFTER PASSING THE Canary Islands, we began a more westerly course. Our plan was to head west on a southward curving trajectory to take full advantage of the prevailing currents and trade winds—light, steady winds that blow westward across the Atlantic. Our route was far from a direct great circle line, but it would allow us to avoid contrary conditions.

A great-circle route is the shortest distance between two points on the Earth. When this line is drawn on a Mercator projection it does not look straight, but curves north in the Northern Hemisphere and south below the equator. Thus, if we took the most direct route to Miami, we would follow a curve, first north of our destination, then slowly going down. The great circle route from Lisbon to Miami extends as far north as Nova Scotia's latitude. Imagine pulling a piece of string tight between two points on a globe; the course the string naturally takes is the great circle route. An extreme example of the great circle concept is the most direct route from Adelaide, Australia, to Rio de Janeiro, Brazil—a course that would go over the South Pole. Or, to take an example from the Northern Hemisphere, the shortest route from Toronto to Bangkok is via the North Pole.

Taking the shortest route would have shaved thousands of kilometres off our crossing, but it might have made the journey impossible and turned us into the rowboat version of The Flying Dutchman—forever forced to row in a sea of opposing winds and currents. Miami is 6,700 kilometres from Lisbon, but we would row between 8,000 and 9,500 kilometres to connect these points. Our pilot charts—a comprehensive compilation of observations from thousands of ships' logs— indicated favourable winds in a southern route. Although the weather had strayed significantly from the averages so far, we hoped it would be more typical from now on.

THE LAST OF the Canary Islands passed to our north, turning into distant blue forms that gradually sank into the sea. We had now diverged from major shipping lanes and rarely saw other vessels; once again, Colin and I were alone with the vast, watery expanse around us. Even though I had Colin to keep me company, the immense solitude was sometimes overwhelming, and I marvelled at those who embarked on long and difficult journeys alone.

Decades earlier John Fairfax had rowed from the Canary Islands to Miami all alone. Fairfax's crossing of the Pacific Ocean with his girlfriend Sylvia in 1971 (when he was bitten by a shark) was actually his second major rowing voyage. In 1969 he left from Gran Canaria (the island we had just passed) and spent six months crossing to Miami in his rowboat, becoming the first to row the Atlantic Ocean from east to west.

His rowboat was much less sophisticated than ours. There was no sealed cabin to escape the foul weather; the waves sloshed right over his bed. Satellite telephone technology didn't exist, and his means of communication was a shortwave radio that didn't work most of the time. Even his freshwater drinking requirements were a logistical nightmare that included a complex still, a rain catchment system, and the odd passing freighter. His odds of completing the journey were probably just as high as his odds of never being found again.

Three years before John Fairfax's attempt, two boats had tried to row across the Atlantic from the U.S. to Europe. One of the boats, *Puffin*, was manned by two journalists under contract from the London newspaper *The People*. *Puffin* was a custom-designed boat fairly well suited to the task, complete with independent flotation chambers, self-righting capabilities, and a small cabin. The other vessel, *English Rose III*, crewed by Englishmen John Ridgway and Chay Blyth, was much more primitive; the men didn't have funds for anything more than a simple open dory.

The media closely followed what had become a race to be the first to row across the Atlantic Ocean in the twentieth century. Unfortunately the crew of *Puffin* succumbed to the forces of the ocean and were never seen again. In September 1966, the Canadian destroyer-escort *Chaudière* located an upturned vessel about 950 kilometres southeast of Newfoundland. It turned out to be *Puffin*, and the boat was retrieved from the water. Several items remained on board, including a ship's log that revealed the crew was getting disheartened on their long voyage. But there was no clue as to what brought about their demise. The final entry on September 3 stated, "No rowing because of north-northwest winds of force two." These light headwinds presumably intensified into a storm with the strength to capsize their vessel, and their water ballast may not have been sufficiently full to right it.

John Ridgway and Chay Blyth, however, fared better in their six-metre open dory. They departed from Cape Cod two weeks after the *Puffin*, using their military training to assist in a relentless schedule of non-stop rowing. Half the day the men would row in tandem, and the other twelve hours they rowed individually. Their vessel was in constant danger of being swamped, and they were often forced to bail frantically with buckets to keep the sea out. After ninety-two days rowing on the frigid North Atlantic, they finally reached the shores of Ireland, exhausted and emaciated.

The British media was frantic to capture the story, and two reporters died in their haste to reach Ridgway and Blyth (one fell off a boat and the other was caught in a plane crash). Their story made the front page of newspapers around the world, and the festivities went on for months. Even Queen Elizabeth II hosted a cocktail party for the triumphant rowers at Buckingham Palace.

John Ridgway is perhaps the best-known ocean rower in the world, and by great coincidence I had the pleasure of meeting him. The previous owners of our rowboat were brothers, Richard and Will Burchnall. Will is John Ridgway's son-in-law, and the rowboat had been stored at Ridgway's adventure retreat on the northwestern shores of Scotland.

The brothers did not row across the Atlantic Ocean as they'd planned and instead put the boat up for sale. They had bought it two years earlier from another British man who, along with a friend, had rowed across the Atlantic from the Canary Islands to the Caribbean. Before them, another team of two men had taken the boat across the Atlantic on a similar route. When I'd been close to finalizing the boat purchase, I travelled to Scotland to inspect the vessel. I flew from Vancouver to London to Inverness, where I rented a stick-shift car and drove on the wrong side of the road until it narrowed into a single lane. The landscape was nothing more than weathered granite with heather huddled into the folds. Old stone crofter's cabins, their roofs sagging, hinted at the resilience of the people who inhabited this wild region. I finally reached Cape Adventure International, a cluster of buildings perched near the water in a sheltered bay. The sea was deep blue, almost black, against a Scottish milky-blue sky.

Will Burchnall led me over pastoral fields and low stone walls to see our future rowboat. *Ondine,* or *Manpower* as she was then named, sat on the side of a gravel road, looking like a broken-down vehicle left to rot on the front lawn of a dishevelled home. I knew that she was nine years old and had been sitting unused for two years, but I somehow envisioned a boat selling for thirty-two thousand dollars would look a little more, well, valuable. I stepped into the boat, crawled inside the cabin, and lay down, imagining what it would be like to be on the ocean in this small vessel.

After I thoroughly inspected Ondine, Will took me across the bay in a small motorboat to John Ridgway's water-access-only home. A fit older man walked down to the wharf to greet us, and I suddenly realized I was looking at Ridgway himself.

In his late sixties, John looked like he could still row across an ocean, and indeed, he has continued to be physically active since his days rowing across the Atlantic. As we walked the grounds around his home, the adventurer described his years of sailing the world and exploring the Amazon.

Finally we reached a large wooden shed. John placed his bony hand on the latch and twisted. The door swung open; inside was his old rowboat, *English Rose III*. It looked no different from the old dories used in Newfoundland for fishing, and I couldn't believe that this little open boat had made it across the Atlantic. I looked up at John with a renewed respect.

"We started with more than a dozen oars," he said with a chuckle, as he pointed to those that remained.

The shafts of the oars looked as though they had been whittled away by a hungry beaver. During their ninety-two-day non-stop row, John and his partner had had no cabin to shelter them from the elements when they slept; they wrapped themselves in blankets and oilskins and lay on the sodden floor.

I couldn't imagine crossing an ocean in that boat.

"This boat wasn't our first choice, but we couldn't afford the one we wanted to use," John said, as if reading my mind.

When John had planned this trip, he was a twenty-six-year-old paratrooper without sponsors or money to buy a boat. His bank gave him an overdraft; the military allowed him unpaid leave, and forty-six days before his departure, he found a partner in fellow paratrooper Chay Blyth. When they left, the coast guard estimated they had a 95 per cent chance of dying. But despite pessimistic predictions, they reached the far shores of the Atlantic Ocean just three months later.

"We're all made pretty much the same," John said. He tapped his index finger to his temple. "It's what's in here that counts." He paused a moment. "And whatever happens, never give up."

At the time I was just thrilled that this accomplished explorer was supportive of my journey, but since then I've thought back frequently to just how true those words were. The biggest challenge on this trip wasn't mustering the physical strength to tackle big waves or continue rowing past the point of exhaustion. It was simply to keep going. To control my fear, doubts, and pessimism, and to continue forward, dealing with the challenges as they arose.

ON OUR THIRTY-FIFTH day at sea, I woke up to discover we had company. A storm petrel had decided our boat made a convenient resting spot and was asleep on the bristle brush we used to tackle the barnacles.

When I stepped onto the deck, the bird woke but didn't move. It was sitting between the rowing tracks, definitely not a safe spot once I started rowing. I gently lifted the bird with the brush and relocated it to a safer place. It wasn't scared as I cradled it in my hands, and I guessed this was a result of having no predators. I hoped an injury was not the cause of its prolonged rest. Storm petrels have evolved to ply the ocean skies for most of their lives, and their legs can barely support the weight of their bodies. As far as I know, they do not commonly land on boats.

Once I started rowing, the petrel realized that its peace had been permanently disrupted and that a return to slumber was impossible. It relinquished its bristle bed and began wandering around the deck, wings flapping in unsuccessful attempts at flight. The deck was too small and cluttered to provide an adequate runway.

Eventually I realized that without help, it would not succeed. I cupped my hands around its body and gently placed the bird on the gunwale. But instead of using this unencumbered space to take off, it promptly strolled onto the oar, scrabbled on the slippery surface, and fell into the water. Pumping its wings, the bird ran along the water's surface for forty metres, but was unable to gain enough lift to fly. When it stopped, it floated low in the water, struggling. This creature was definitely not designed for swimming, and I hoped I hadn't unwittingly aided in its demise. I steered the boat closer, hoping to provide some assistance. The bird tried a second time, pumping and flapping and running for perhaps fifty metres. Finally it lifted from the ocean's surface to freedom, and disappeared into the distance.

Later that day we were visited by more petrels. They circled our boat, flying low, skimming the water's surface, and tapping it rhythmically with their feet. Although we'd seen petrels before, this was the first time they'd tap-danced for us, and the biological purpose of this behaviour became a hot topic of conversation. Later research on the birds revealed little as to what purpose this pattering serves, apart from possibly helping to stabilize the creatures as they hover near the surface to feed. The petrels skimmed near the surface of the water, pattering and dipping their wingtips into the water as they scooped up copepods and other small crustaceans with their beaks.

It looked like they were walking on water, so we nicknamed them "Jesus birds." Little did we know that our label was far from original. We later found out that "petrel" is a diminutive form of the name Peter, as in Saint Peter, the biblical apostle who walked on water (albeit briefly). We did not know that then, nor did we know that the "storm" in storm petrel came from the birds' tendency to hide in the lee of ships when tempests approached and that they are considered harbingers of winds and waves.

ON OCTOBER 28, water and sky shared a steely grey hue. Before sunrise the ocean was a glassy calm, but by early morning a gentle ripple caressed its surface. By 10:00 AM scattered whitecaps dotted the sea and the waves increased to two metres in height. The winds were against us, increasing in speed until they blew from the west at thirty kilometres an hour.

I worked hard, lengthening my oar stroke, increasing the pace, pushing hard with my legs, and digging my oars into the water, but my efforts were in vain. We barely moved. The measly half-horsepower I could exert was nothing compared to the ocean's forces. I thought of the millions of stationary rowing machines in gyms around the world and tried to console myself that I wasn't the only person rowing on the spot. But when the gym rowers stop, they go relax in the sauna. If I stopped we just drifted backwards and lost precious ground.

I hated this. I wanted to quit, to cry uncle, to stomp my feet in a tantrum against the cruel gods of the sea. I wanted to moan to Colin about how much I loathed this, to wallow in my own dissatisfaction. But I didn't. I kept my mouth shut and continued rowing, because it wouldn't make a difference. The emotionless ocean bends for no one.

I was glad I had stopped myself from complaining to Colin; it would have darkened the mood on the boat. I tried to achieve inner peace with our situation, but all I could think about was how hard I was working and how little we were moving. It was hard to believe the end would ever be in sight. At this moment the journey was the antithesis of instant gratification. I forced myself to think ahead to the days when our row across the Atlantic Ocean would be a tale we would share with our grandchildren, when the storms and headwinds would be nothing but punctuation for a rich memory. After all, aren't struggles, hardships, and failures ultimately overshadowed by success?

It seems ironic that the goals that appear so intimidating, complex, and glorious are often composed of simple, mundane activities. Pulling on oars in the ocean is not difficult in itself; the challenge is to stay steadfast and committed in the face of adversity. I thought again of what John Ridgway had said: *It's all up here.* That's true for most objectives in life. It's not talent that ensures success, but commitment and perseverance.

Easy enough to say, but our levels of perseverance were running low. After a frustrating eight hours of rowing nowhere, we finally gave up. Colin cut his rowing shift short and instead we trailed a rope and chain to slow our drift. We both settled into the cabin and drifted backwards, slowly losing the hard-won progress gained earlier in the day. Colin called Dean Fenwick, our coordinator, on the satellite phone for the latest weather forecast, and the news was good. In twenty-four hours the winds were forecast to switch around to the northeast, and they would be in our favour.

But the headwinds would not let up until two days later, so we spent little time rowing. Instead we lay in the cabin, and Colin worked on his book *Beyond the Horizon* while I read Farley Mowat's *A Whale for the Killing.*

Mowat has long been one of my favourite authors, and this book is especially compelling, a true story of the sad fate of a pilot whale that became stranded in a tiny bay in New-foundland. The whale pursued a school of fish through the shallow entrance of the bay during an exceptionally high tide, but once the tide ebbed, the creature's exit disappeared. The gentle giant became a source of unwanted attention from the local villagers, who chased the whale in speedboats and used it for rifle target practice. Pocked with countless bullet holes and wounded by a boat propeller, it eventually died from its infected injuries. That was in 1967, and thankfully societal views towards whales have improved since then.

Many whale populations have rebounded since the mora-torium on commercial whaling; some, such as the grey whale, have returned from the verge of extinction. The pilot whale, once hunted ferociously, is now one of the most abundant and widespread cetaceans. So far we had spotted what we thought were two pilot whales, but sadly neither had come very close to our boat.

"TRICK OR TREAT. Our fortieth day at sea is Halloween, and we've been treated to northeast winds at force four! We're moving at 1.8 to 2.5 knots, and our spirits are high," I wrote in my journal.

It was a wonderful change, and these conditions were forecast to persist all week. It finally looked like we would make some decent progress. Perhaps this was the start of the famous trade winds.

"I'm afraid I forgot to pack our Halloween costumes," I joked.

"You can dress up as a mermaid and I'll be a pirate," Colin said.

"You already look like a pirate," I said.

All Colin needed was an eye patch. His hair had not been cut since he'd left Vancouver seventeen months before. It now reached his shoulders, a far cry from his usual crew cut, while his bushy beard enveloped the lower half of his face. Had I not seen the transformation in slow motion, I might have had difficulty recognizing him.

I, however, looked no different. My hair was a little more knotted and my face sunburned, but that was about it.

"Well, if we do get any visitors . . . I know one treat we could offer," Colin said pointing to the lure on our fishing rod.

"That would be a *trick*."

"That depends on your perspective," said Colin.

left: The deck of the rowboat, showing the two rowing seats, circular hatches, and bow storage compartment.

PHOTO: COLIN ANGUS

below: Showing off a dorado caught mid-Atlantic.

PHOTO: COLIN ANGUS

A typical day
rowing on the ocean.

PHOTO: COLIN ANGUS

A larger-than-usual
dorado we caught that
provided several meals.

PHOTO: JULIE ANGUS

Sun-drying dorado fish that we caught mid-Atlantic—delicious in soup. PHOTO: JULIE ANGUS

Eating a special dinner of dorado, rice, and vegetables on the rowboat. PHOTO: COLIN ANGUS

A loggerhead turtle that took a keen interest in our boat and in the barnacles growing on our hull.

Colin rowing towards St. Lucia, after being on the ocean for four months.

Rowing near St. Lucia in the Caribbean, after travelling more than seven thousand kilometres from Portugal. PHOTO: KIRK ELLIOT

Sitting inside the cabin while moored in St. Lucia. PHOTO: ANGUS ADVENTURES

above: Celebrating
our arrival in
St. Lucia after
rowing from
Lisbon, Portugal.

PHOTO: ANGUS
ADVENTURES

right: One of
the Costa Rican
newspaper articles
that covered
our journey.

PHOTO: COLIN ANGUS

Reaching Port Limón on the east coast of Costa Rica
after rowing ten thousand kilometres from Lisbon, Portugal.

Celebrating the completion of the expedition in Vancouver after cycling 8,300 kilometres from Costa Rica. PHOTO: ANGUS ADVENTURES

Hiking along the Puntledge River, near our home on Vancouver Island, after completing the expedition. PHOTO: JULIE ANGUS

10

ENCOUNTERS WITH A
LOVESTRUCK TURTLE

ISTANCE TAKES ON a different meaning when you move through a landscape that never changes. On the open ocean, only a gently curving horizon cuts a line between blue sky and cerulean sea. There is nothing to indicate forward progress, no milestones to check off—just a hope that the GPS is accurate. Nothing on terra firma can compare; even the most unchanging lands offer slight aberrations—hills, shrubs, dunes, rocks—to be used for reference.

Our lives were now governed by firmly established, unchanging routines, and the days swallowed each other, each one shaped from the same cookie cutter. We rowed for twenty hours and travelled between fifty and eighty kilometres. The weather was warm, the winds not too strong, and the sky was sunny, dotted with fluffy, innocent clouds. Sporadically, we saw tuna, dorado, and flying fish; occasionally we were visited by dolphins or whales. Our conversations revolved around the mundane as well as the philosophical.

Conditions were better now, but our overall progress was far from ideal. In forty-nine days, we had rowed only one-quarter of the distance to Miami. If we continued at this speed, our supplies would be depleted long before reaching land.

Two days before—nine days after leaving the Canary Islands—the weather had briefly taken a peculiar turn. A thick cloud cover created a dark, shadowy world, and a dense haze reduced our visibility to just two or three kilometres. I wondered if it was created by fine sand being blown out to sea from the deserts of Africa, a phenomenon we'd read about in our pilot book. Our speed dropped by 40 per cent, and we faced steeper swells with shorter wavelengths.

"It's the currents," Colin said, looking at the GPS. "They're no longer flowing southwest, but have reversed, pushing straight into the winds. When the winds and currents are not unified, they create a wind-over-current situation, which creates choppy seas."

"Why would the currents and winds flow in different directions?" I asked. "I thought surface currents were created by the winds."

"That's usually the case. Generally, currents are created by prevailing winds, but the water can continue flowing great distances from momentum, even pushing into contrary conditions as it is now. Based on the information in our charts, though, it's not common for currents to flow northward here."

The boat rocked violently in the steep waves, and for the first time in weeks, I felt queasy. We had to continue rowing hard to move out of this strong current. But we had no way of knowing where the edges of the flow lay. The great, fluid movements of the ocean are constantly changing, and satellite technology does not have the means to detect ocean currents. We could only hope to bumble our way along.

We decided to clean the bottom of the boat to help increase our speed. It was my turn, but a splitting headache all but incapacitated me. So I kept watch, and Colin jumped overboard with the mask and snorkel to scrape the barnacles. He gripped the safety line with one hand and rubbed off crustaceans with the other. The boat bounced wildly in the waves, and I worried the hull would hit him.

"I can't believe how fast these guys grow," Colin said as he surfaced between dives.

"Just be quick," I said. "It's hard to see in these choppy waters." I scanned the horizon and the water beneath the boat for sharks. My polarizing sunglasses helped cut what little glare was on the surface, but visibility was still poor.

Colin submerged again. I squinted—nothing in the distance, nothing under the boat. What if a shark snuck up? What if I didn't see it? The risk just didn't seem worth it. Colin had already been in the water for ten minutes scraping off hundreds of barnacles, meaty morsels that rained into the ocean depths like the ringing of a dinner bell to all predators. I turned to scan the waters behind me, and a dark shadow flickered.

"SHARK!" I screamed. "Get in the boat, now!"

Colin shot to the surface and got into the boat in one fluid motion. He was panting, and blood dripped from a scratch on his thigh.

"Are you okay?" I asked, pointing to his leg.

"I'm fine," he said. "It's nothing."

Colin's reaction time had been incredibly quick. Instead of getting into the boat as he usually did, by grabbing the railing and pulling himself up—which would have left his legs dangling in the water for precious moments longer—he had thrown his legs onto the boat first and quickly pulled himself out of the water. The cut was from where he'd rubbed against the boat's metal oarlock.

"Where is it?" he asked.

"Over there," I said, pointing to a now-empty area of water. "It was about a metre and a half long and just off the starboard side."

We scanned the water for a sign of the shark, but found none.

"Maybe it wasn't a shark after all," I said sheepishly. "I just saw it out of the corner of my eye."

"I'd much rather you to be wrong about seeing a shark than wait another minute to confirm that a shark is sizing me up."

"I don't think you should scrape the hull anymore," I said.

"At least not today," Colin agreed.

Colin dried off and went into the cabin. I started rowing.

"Hey, your scraping job did the trick. We're going faster than before—about 0.3 to 0.5 knots faster," I said, watching the speed reading on the GPS.

"That's great," he replied. "I only cleaned off about half of them."

"Now that you mention it, we seem to be tracking a little more to the starboard side. That was the side you didn't scrape, right?"

Colin looked at me with dismay.

"Just kidding."

"IT'S TED AND FRED!" Colin suddenly shouted.

He dropped the oars and peered over the side of the boat. I quickly joined him to view two fish swimming off our portside.

"Are you sure they're Ted and Fred?" I asked.

"It sure looks like them. Look at their stripes. That one there with the scar is Fred, and remember Ted's ripped tail— that looks just like him. Maybe they were following our boat from a distance, or somehow they tracked us down again."

I wasn't entirely convinced. The fish certainly did look like Ted and Fred, but why hadn't we seen them all this time? And where were Ned and Oscar? I searched the surrounding waters, but there was no sign of the other half of the quartet. I was excited to have a couple of pets again, and who knows, maybe it *was* them. I tossed a few spoons of leftover rice and corn over the side for the hungry fish.

TED AND FRED had rejoined us just as we were about to enter the tropics and cross the tropic of Cancer, the latitudinal meridian that lies at 23°26 north, approximately 2,600 kilometres north of the equator.

"Let's have a party to celebrate being in the tropics," Colin said.

"Sounds great. I think we should drink the wine that Mario gave us with tonight's dinner," I said.

Though we were happy to be in the tropics, things didn't look any more tropical. The weather had been in the mid-twenties for a long time now, and the sea was just as blue and empty as always. The waves were still choppy, and the currents continued to come from a suboptimal direction. But it was still an exciting moment, and I was glad it wouldn't slip by unnoticed, swallowed by another nondescript day rowing.

"Did I ever tell you the story about when we crossed the equator in the *Virginian?*" Colin said, his eyes glazing over as he remembered his heady years sailing.

"You mean the time you pierced your ear with a potato and a needle?"

"That's it," Colin said, mildly disappointed. "How about when we went up on a reef in Palau in poorly charted waters?"

Colin retold his story while we searched for exciting dinner ingredients. Our food selection was getting pretty slim. It was now day fifty-two, and we had almost finished the food set aside for the first half of the journey. We would soon need to access the second half, which was stored in separate storage compartments.

"How about some American cookies to start the party?" I said, rummaging through the food pile that now sat on the mattress in our cabin. Chocolate chip cookies with an "American" label were our favourites, along with sour candies and canned lychee fruit.

"You bet," Colin said enthusiastically. He set down the oars and stretched out his hand for the treats.

Our food shopping in Lisbon had been a rushed affair, and we'd been unfamiliar with many of the products. Now, in the middle of the ocean, we quickly learned the difference between good and disgusting. Unfortunately, we had no choice but to eat everything.

The "American cookies" turned out to be the best treat on board. Unfortunately, the very name had put us off buying too many of these biscuits. I had assumed they were full of preservatives and heavily processed. In fact, the Portuguese-made goodies contained all-natural ingredients and tasted as though they were fresh from grandma's oven. If they'd labelled them "Portuguese Cookies" or "All-Natural Cookies," we probably would have purchased several dozen more packages. Instead, we had enough only for special occasions, such as birthdays and crossing the tropic of Cancer.

I gave Colin three cookies and took three more for myself. We'd eat the remaining six tonight, before they softened in the moisture-laden air.

"Mmmm," Colin said, his face an expression of joy.

Colin finished his cookies in a few bites between oar strokes. I nibbled mine slowly, willing them to last as long as possible, while I pondered what to make for dinner. I had soaked dried chickpeas in water overnight, so I decided on a vegetarian version of the Moroccan chicken I make at home—a baked dish of browned onions, chickpeas, raisins, and chicken in a medley of Middle Eastern spices. Unfortunately, we didn't have an oven, chicken, or most of the required spices. But with a few modifications, almost any recipe can be adapted to a rowboat galley.

So here is my version of Moroccan Chicken, rowboat-style. Thinly slice half an onion and sauté it in olive oil. Sprinkle sugar on the onions after they have browned, and continue cooking until the sugar caramelizes but before it burns. (On a rowboat, brown sugar is preferred. While white sugar absorbs moisture and turns into a solid block, brown sugar stays soft and moist.) Add one cup of chicken broth, four cups of softened chickpeas, and a handful of raisins. Simmer until the chickpeas are cooked and the liquid is mostly absorbed. Add salt, pepper, and a pinch of cinnamon. Serve on a bed of rice or couscous.

We celebrated our progress and official entrance to the tropics in a boat that smelled like the kitchen of a Middle Eastern restaurant. I heaped large helpings of curry and couscous onto our plastic plates, and filled our mugs with wine. The sky blazed with pinpricks of light—millions of stars to remind us that we were just tiny specks in the universe. I could see the Big Dipper clearly in the northern sky, looking just as it had from my bedroom window in Edmonton when I stared at the constellations as a little girl.

"That's the Southern Cross," Colin said, pointing to an area low in the southern horizon.

I searched the sky for the telltale five stars that make up the constellation and finally found it. The four brightest stars can be connected to create a cross, like the four corners of a kite. The Southern Cross is one of the most prominent celestial features in the Southern Hemisphere and, since ancient times, has been used by sailors for navigation. It serves a similar purpose to the North Star, or polestar, in the Northern Hemisphere.

We finished the bottle of wine under the star-filled sky, waves lapping gently against the boat and a warm breeze caressing us. Ted and Fred illuminated the phosphorescence as they splashed around the boat. Colin's arms were wrapped around me, and life seemed perfect. I couldn't imagine a more romantic night.

THUMP... BANG... THUD...It was 5:30 AM, and the noise reverberated through the hull of the boat. Something was banging against it. At first I thought the ropes securing the rudder had loosened and that the rudder was being slammed against the boat. But the noise was too loud and irregular to be the rudder. When I climbed out of bed to investigate, the racket suddenly stopped. I paused, listening intently. *Bang.* This time it was terrifyingly loud. I lunged out the main hatch while Colin squeezed through the smaller roof hatch.

"The rudder looks okay," Colin yelled from the back. "The lines are a little frayed, but everything's still . . ."

BANG

The noise came from the starboard side. I clambered to the edge, expecting to see a log or other oceanic debris. Instead I stared straight into the large, round eyes of a giant sea turtle. It was about a metre in diameter, accompanied by an entourage of small grey and black striped fish, miniature versions of Fred and Ted.

"It's an enormous turtle!" I shouted.

During the voyage up to that point, we had seen dozens of turtles, but they were all tiny in comparison, and shier than blushing schoolgirls. They would edge up to investigate, but quickly turn tail as soon as Colin or I moved in a manner unbecoming of a piece of flotsam. Our newest visitor wasn't shy at all, and was obviously unperturbed by my nearness or even the way the tumultuous waters were heaving our vessel up and down onto its hard shell with a thump.

"I see it," Colin said as he leaned out the roof hatch, holding the video camera. "He's doing a great job cleaning the bottom of the boat. We'll be sliding through the water after he's done with us."

While Colin filmed, I took photographs. The turtle's leathery neck protruded two hand-lengths from its fortified home. Its beak, which looked capable of snapping a finger in half, effortlessly nipped off the inch-long barnacles. Its long flippers swept through the water as it scrabbled against our boat to graze. Its carapace was shades of brown—the archetypal tortoise-shell coloration—and made up of multiple plates strong enough to protect it from most predators, including mid-sized sharks.

This was a loggerhead turtle. We knew that five species of sea turtle inhabited this part of the Atlantic Ocean—green, Kemp's ridley, leatherback, hawksbill, and loggerhead—and until then, we had only seen hawksbill turtles. Because of our visitor's blunt jaws and long flippers, we knew it wasn't a hawksbill, which looks quite similar except for its sharp, pointed beak and two claws at the tip of each flipper. This turtle's size was also a giveaway. We guessed it would tip the scales at 250 kilograms, several times heavier than the largest hawksbill, and would dwarf those we had seen several hundred kilometres off the coast of Africa (which were never larger than a bicycle tire). Although we hadn't yet spotted the other types, we knew from our reference book that they looked quite different than this one.

If size was any indication, our turtle was a geriatric, which in turtle years is only forty or fifty. She or he (I couldn't tell) was drifting on the ocean currents looking for food and perhaps en route to a warmer place for winter. Unlike other sea turtles, loggerheads even searched for love along their migration routes, and we hoped our new friend wouldn't mistake our boat for an amorous mate. But then, mating season was only between March and June, and it was November. More likely this turtle had already gotten lucky and, if it was a female, had laid her eggs in a hole she dug on a Mediterranean beach a few months before. By then her clutch of 100 to 120 eggs would have hatched, and the young would have waddled to the water under the cloak of darkness to make their way to safer grounds.

The sea turtle lives a dangerous life. Only a fraction survive beyond their first year, and far fewer return to the area where they were born to breed. When young they are vulnerable to natural predators, but even as they mature, the risks are great, especially from humans. Their meat and eggs are considered a delicacy, their shells a beautiful material for ornaments, and their fat a product for cosmetics and medicine. All seven species of sea turtles, including the five living in this part of the Atlantic, are classified as threatened or endangered. It is now illegal to hunt sea turtles in most countries. However, turtles still face dangers from boat propellers, fishing nets, longline fishing hooks, disruption of nesting grounds, and illegal hunting.

The plight of sea turtles has garnered global attention, and ongoing efforts are making a difference in their survival. Changes in fishing practices—using slightly different hooks or bait, and nets that turtles can escape from—has led to a 97 per cent reduction in turtle by-catch by vessels that adopt the practices. In Florida, concerned groups dig up turtle eggs at risk of being trampled by beachgoers and rebury them in secure fenced-off areas. Conservationists in Central America monitor nesting sites to prevent poaching. "Don't Eat Sea Turtle" awareness campaigns have been created to target the black market trade in turtle products. But turtles mature slowly, have offspring infrequently, and live long lives. It will take time for their populations to rebound.

"I'm worried about our boat," Colin said as another thump reverberated through our vessel. "How much abuse can quarter-inch plywood take?"

"That would be an unfortunate end to our expedition. But it would make a great headline. 'Boat holed by lovestruck turtle.'"

My comment was punctuated by a splintering crash.

"Maybe it's time we moved on."

I untied the oars and started rowing.

"He's chasing us," Colin yelled. "Row faster!"

I put all my strength into the oars and laughed at the absurdity of our situation. We were trying to escape an overly affectionate turtle. Of all the dangers I envisioned prior to setting off, this one was not on the list.

"I'm exhausted," I said, after the turtle finally tired and disappeared astern. I lifted the oars from the water for a break.

"You can't stop now," Colin said, his voice filled with dismay. "Don't you remember what happened with the tortoise and the hare? He's probably plodding along straight towards us, and any second he's going to crash through the bottom of the boat."

ELEVEN DAYS HAD passed since we'd crossed the tropic of Cancer, and the trade winds should have blown steadily. Instead the winds were variable, frequently changing direction and often dead calm.

As we struggled westward, a black wall of clouds appeared on the horizon ahead of us. The blue sky contrasted sharply with the ragged, undulating mass in the distance. Hours slipped by, but the system did not move.

At night we could see an almost continual diffused flashing light in the horizon, created by heavy electrostatic activity in the distant clouds. The lightning was too far away to hear. I felt somewhat uneasy witnessing such a phenomenal release of energy while we sat upon a calm ocean. The stars above us twinkled, and a five-knot wind blew from the north.

We rowed through most of the night. Morning light revealed a world that had changed little from the previous day. Above us and to the east, the sky was a rich blue scattered with innocent puffs of cloud. To the west towered foreboding thunderheads, a wall of shovelled coal smouldering and ready to explode.

Generally, storm systems or squalls move across the ocean at speeds of ten to fifty knots, which means, from the perspective of a boat, that they are a rapidly moving entity. The squall system we were looking at, however, sat on the same spot, growing in strength and intensity. We could see the clouds rising in height and the frequency of lightning increasing. It ran in a continuous line as far north and south as we could see. Only our own slow progress of about two knots slowly closed the gap between us and the system. We guessed the storm to be about fifty nautical miles away, so if it remained stationary, we would still take another two days to reach it.

That evening we were treated to another light show. This time we could hear the thunder, a continual throaty rumbling. It never ceased, only fluctuated in intensity. Even the lightning itself was almost non-stop. We didn't see bolts of lightning; instead, different parts of the cloud formation lit up, and every detail of the anvil head became clear from internal illumination.

The storm looked sinister, and, even more unnerving, it wasn't moving. It cut like a felt marker across the sky, and we continuously advanced towards it.

"Maybe we should stop rowing, or even go in the other direction," Colin suggested.

"I don't know. It just seems that would be prolonging the inevitable," I said. "It has to start moving at some point, and when it does, it will go east. It might even be more intense by that time. Plus, we'll lose a lot of precious ground."

"I guess," Colin said, shrugging his shoulders. "There's always the possibility it might just die out. But you're probably right; we should just charge through it and get it over with."

As we continued rowing towards the storm, it was hard not to feel like we were voluntarily heading towards our own doom.

It took two more days of rowing to reach the wall of darkness. At 1:00 PM the sun slipped behind the clouds, and the world dimmed like a sudden solar eclipse. The light northeast winds ceased, and the air became still. Within minutes the air temperature dropped ten to fifteen degrees. Even though I was rowing hard, I felt cold. There was no wind, but violent, confused waves buffeted our boat and made it hard to row. Colin said the turbulent waves were caused by heavy winds blowing nearby.

Finally, my shift ended. I wished Colin good luck, climbed into the cabin, and locked the door.

"We've got to row as quickly as possible, no matter how rough it gets," Colin shouted from outside. "This thing isn't moving, and the only way we'll cross through to the other side is under our own steam."

Colin started rowing and, as we approached the thunderheads, the wind suddenly intensified. It was though a switch had been flipped; the wind speed went from zero to about forty knots. The wind blew straight towards the centre of the storm.

"I've gone from 3 to 5.5 knots," Colin screamed from outside.

He struggled to keep the boat from broaching. I watched him through the rain-splattered Plexiglas window. His muscles bulged as he forced one oar forward and the other back. Lesser oars would have snapped under the strain, and almost anyone else would have given up.

The ocean had turned white with spray. Waves came from multiple directions and often collided into each other, shooting plumes of water tens of metres into the air. All around us, lightning flashed and winds shrieked. A few minutes before, the ocean had been dead calm, and now it looked like Hollywood animation for the film *The Perfect Storm*. We had passed through the black wall into an evil world. Hopefully it wasn't a one-way ticket.

"I CAN'T KEEP IT STRAIGHT ANYMORE! THESE WINDS ARE HURRICANE-FORCE!" Colin screamed.

The boat turned sideways to the waves, water crashed over the cabin, and our forward momentum slowed to a crawl. If Colin couldn't pivot the boat to face into the wind and waves, our chances of capsizing skyrocketed, and there was no telling when we would get out of there. But Colin persevered and eventually his efforts were rewarded. We accelerated forward, the waves once again providing more of a push than a pounding.

Suddenly, the wind slowed, and the rain intensified. Colin was now rowing in calmer conditions, but under the heaviest deluge I have ever seen. The torrential downpour helped subdue the tumultuous seas. Lightning still crackled and flashed, and the level of illumination permeating the clouds was no more than that of a moonlit night. Though only two metres away, I couldn't hear Colin through the noise of the constant thunder and drumming rain.

He knocked on the hatch. It was my shift now. I put on my waterproof Helly Hansen rain gear and scrambled out into what felt like the inside of a waterfall. Colin flopped into the cabin, exhausted from his intense two-hour marathon.

The blackness, the torrents, and the lightning continued through my shift, but now it felt more invigorating than terrifying. I rowed through the deluge, and near the end of my shift, the sky began to lighten. The proverbial silver lining had appeared in the western sky. As we neared the perimeter of the squall line, the rain slowed and the winds intensified. It was a delicate balance keeping the boat on course in strong winds; the slightest deviation was amplified by the twisting forces of the wind and waves. I was at the limits of my capabilities, exhausted and barely able to keep the boat under control in the buffeting winds. But finally we passed through the squall line.

The weather on the other side stood in stark contrast to the blue skies and fluffy clouds east of the squall line: an unsettled mix of towering thunderheads, wispy cirrus, and churning cumulonimbus. The setting sun projected great shafts of fiery light between the clouds.

"Thank God it's over," Colin said. "I've been dreading that for days."

"If our water-maker was broken, we could have collected enough fresh water for the entire voyage in there."

Colin peered into an upturned bucket that was half-full of rainwater. "It looks like twenty centimetres of rain fell."

"Do you think something weird is going on?" I asked.

"I don't know, but I think we should call Dean and have him check the weather forecast. This weather still looks pretty strange."

Colin went into the cabin to phone Dean, and I went back to rowing. I heard Colin's side of the conversation through the open hatch.

"Hey, Deano. We're having some really odd weather here and were wondering if you could check the Hurricane Center website to confirm that there are no hurricanes in the region."

There was a pause while Dean looked up the information online. I scrutinized Colin's expression, waiting for the relaxed look that would appear when Dean joked about what weather-chondriacs we were. But that didn't happen. Instead, Colin's face remained tight. Then he finally asked, "What direction is it heading in?"

My stomach dropped.

Colin closed the satellite phone and relayed the news. Tropical Storm Delta had just formed in the middle of the Atlantic, about two thousand kilometres northwest of us. For the National Hurricane Center to call it a tropical storm meant that it had all the features of a hurricane—an eye of low pressure and spiralling winds—but that its wind speed was not yet hurricane-force. If the winds of Tropical Storm Delta intensified to 120 kilometres an hour, Delta would be a hurricane.

I just couldn't believe it was happening again. It was almost the end of hurricane season, and we were still in a part of the Atlantic that rarely saw hurricanes or tropical storms. I couldn't help but feel Mother Nature had a vendetta against us.

Originally, Delta was predicted to travel west, possibly hitting Miami. Inexplicably, and to our dismay, it headed in the opposite direction. Now it had grown in strength and was on the verge of becoming a hurricane. Dean kept us informed of the storm's progress, and we also called the National Hurricane Center directly for additional information. Each time we called the Hurricane Center, they were always professional and precise, never showing any surprise at getting a call from a couple in a rowboat or at the unusual hurricane season. But in their written comments, which were posted online and which we read upon completing the row, we realized that they often shared our frustrated sentiments. "The 2005 Atlantic tropical cyclone season refuses to end," they said when Delta formed—exactly what we thought, but far from what we wanted to hear.

When we had passed through the almost impenetrable squall line, our feelings of being sucked into a black hole weren't entirely unfounded. The bank of unmoving thunderheads heralded a new world of confused and violent weather, the chaos fuelling Delta. When the squall line had appeared three days before, Delta was on the other side, morphing from an extratropical low into something more sinister. Now we were on the wrong side of the line, cozying up to a tropical storm.

We waited nervously for updates from the Hurricane Center, hoping that the storm would veer west or north or even east. But instead, it continued moving towards us. On November 24, the storm slowed down, almost ceasing its forward movement. It remained there for many hours, as if trying to make up its spinning mind. The eye of the storm was only eight hundred kilometres away, and winds were already buffeting us at fifty kilometres an hour.

We launched into the now-familiar routine of preparing *Ondine* for rough seas. We lashed the oars down and stowed all loose gear securely below decks. Colin and I retreated to the protection of the cabin.

Finally, we received some good news from the Hurricane Center. They expected the storm to recurve and move to the northeast—a direction that would take it farther away from us. But, knowing the unpredictability of such intense storms, we felt only nominally reassured. And sure enough, Delta defied these predictions. When it started moving—at the rapid pace of thirty-eight kilometres an hour—it did so in the exact opposite direction of what the Hurricane Center anticipated. Delta still wasn't heading towards us, but we knew it probably wouldn't continue on a southward trajectory for long. Soon it would recurve, as most south-headed storms in this region did, and that would be bad news for us.

All day on November 25, we lay listlessly in the cabin, seeking shelter from the enormous waves buffeting our boat. As the winds shrieked outside, we slid back and forth across the plastic mattress. A strong current, most likely generated by the winds of the nearing tropical storm, moved our boat at a speed of 2.5 knots northeast. Discomfort and fear prevented me from sleeping, and at 6:00 AM, I called the Hurricane Center for the latest forecast.

The news was bad. Delta had stopped its southward march and had now curved to a west-northwest trajectory. Once again a storm was moving straight towards us. This time, however, only seven hundred kilometres sat between us and the eye of the storm, and that distance was quickly shrinking.

Colin and I continued to lay in the cabin, which was dark except for a grey, diffused light from outside. We analyzed Delta's coordinates for hours, trying to come up with reasons why the storm might change track. In reality, however, it wasn't likely. We readied ourselves for the inevitable.

Like Hurricane Vince, the brunt of this storm would arrive in the night. I watched with dismay as the light drained from the sky. Colin and I didn't talk much that night. This was our second named storm, and I was beginning to believe that *Ondine* really did have the capabilities to withstand anything. At about 1:00 AM, the storm escalated, and we thumped against the padded walls of the cabin as waves crashed against and on top of *Ondine*. I was exhausted, yet sleep mostly eluded me. Rest came in short bursts, interrupted by thundering waves or unexplained thumps that warned of our boat's fragility. The storm abated in the early hours of the morning, and finally, I fell asleep. When I awoke, just before dawn, the wind still roared and the waves continued to wash over the deck, but it was better than during the night.

We hoped the worst was over, but we weren't certain until after our call to Dean. Delta had passed and was continuing eastward. We later found out from Colin's mother that Delta went on to kill nineteen people in the Canary Islands. The storm made headlines both because of the destruction it caused, and because meteorologists deemed it "historic."

Tropical storms rarely reach the Canary Islands. It seemed that anomalous weather was becoming commonplace this year.

BEFORE LEAVING LAND, we had worried about hurricanes and storms, but even in our most pessimistic predictions, we never expected such ferocious weather. In Lisbon we had watched news reports of the death and destruction of Hurricane Katrina in horror, and we worried for our own safety. Little did we know the severity of the storms to come, or that this year would go on to be the worst hurricane season in history—breaking not only the record for the most hurricanes in a season, but the most intense (Wilma), the costliest (Katrina), the longest-lasting in December (Epsilon), the longest-lasting in January (Zeta), the second-latest-forming (Zeta), the most eastern-forming (Vince), and the only season with four category-five storms.

The sheer number of hurricanes and the destruction of these storms raised many questions about the relationship between hurricanes and climate change. Few dispute that ocean temperatures have risen and that hurricanes are now more intense and numerous, but how much of that change is due to global warming caused by human activity is hotly debated.

Long after we reached the other side of the ocean, scientists determined that in the year we rowed across the Atlantic, its surface temperature, in the regions where hurricanes form during hurricane season, was at a record high. At home, I read a 2006 article published by National Center for Atmospheric Research scientists Kevin Trenberth and Dennis J. Shea in the journal *Geophysical Research Letters* that detailed these findings. Not only did they determine that the temperature was o.9 degrees Celsius higher than it had been from 1901 to 1970, but that half that spike was linked to global warming. Natural fluctuations could account for only a portion of the temperature increase that was "a major reason for the record hurricane season."

As we rowed through Tropical Storm Delta, we suspected that our changing climate had played a role in the increased tempestuousness of the seas, but only afterwards, when we read the research reports, were we sure.

EVEN IN THESE rough conditions, we still saw fish, birds, and turtles. As we rowed in the chop left in Delta's wake, I saw the silver glimmer of tuna breaking the water's surface and a turtle eyeing our boat from a distance. We were intrigued that even in the wildest weather, these creatures can submerge a few metres to a calm and quiet world. Birds don't have this luxury, and although some depart when they sense an approaching storm, others remain. I watched in wonder as two shearwaters soared across the sky effortlessly, seeming to revel in the wind currents created by the tempest. Their outstretched wings captured invisible updrafts. They gained elevation with barely a wing-flap and occasionally lost altitude to plunge into the ocean after a fish.

11

OUR SECOND MID-ATLANTIC
BIRTHDAY PARTY

O N NOVEMBER 29, Colin turned 34. It was also day
sixty-nine. While Colin rowed in the sweaty heat, I
prepared his birthday cake. I placed a layer of rum-
and-coffee-soaked ladyfinger biscuits across the bottom of a
large pot, then covered it with tapioca pudding made from
dried tapioca, full-fat powdered milk, sugar, and vanilla fla-
vouring. I then slathered strawberry jam from our last jar over
the tapioca, followed by another layer of ladyfingers, and I
topped it all off with whipped cream from a Tetra Pak and
five birthday candles.

I lit the candles and sang "Happy Birthday." The cake was
hardly a secret, as the rowing position faced directly into the
cabin. Nonetheless, Colin feigned surprise.

"Oh my goodness, I thought you were cooking dinner over
there," he said, beaming from ear to ear. "Don't let Michael
Jackson hear you singing that, otherwise he'll be asking for
royalties."

"We'd be paying him in fish," I said, momentarily thinking about our dismal finances.

"Don't worry, he won't find us out here."

Colin closed his eyes, blew out the candles, and then heaped a portion onto his plate.

"Man, this is tasty," he said through a mouthful of cake. "How did you make this after so many months out at sea? It tastes like something you'd get in a gourmet restaurant."

"Maybe I'll start a rowboat cookbook," I said with a laugh.

Colin didn't tell me his wish, but I suspected it involved the weather. This topic dominated our lives; we made daily predictions based mostly on optimism. The success of our expedition was largely reliant on the weather. I reflected back to my birthday wish and shivered. Colin's luck would have to be better than mine. At the very least, I knew it couldn't bring on another hurricane; hurricane season was officially over. In all of history, only five hurricanes have ever formed in December.

Today was the first sunny day in over a week. Fluffy clouds dotted the sky, waves ceased breaking over the decks, and the mercury soared. Even though our speed was slow and the winds variable, we rowed merrily, happy to be free of the cabin confines. Emerging from Tropical Storm Delta gave us a brighter outlook, the way a brush with death can make a person appreciate life.

In the waters near us, dozens of fish jostled for position, some swimming frantically to keep up, others gliding effortlessly. Fred and Ted had made friends, and lots of them. Perhaps our exceptionally slow travel over the past week had raised our curb appeal, or maybe the creatures just enjoyed the security of a larger "mothership" during stormy seas. We counted at least five different species as we stared into the clear waters, marvelling at our no-maintenance aquarium.

The smallest were no larger than goldfish and had golden yellow colouring. During Tropical Storm Delta, we had lowered our makeshift drogue into the ocean, where it sank to a depth of several metres, filled with water, and stabilized our boat. While submerged, it must have attracted the attention of these fish, because when I pulled up the drogue, two dozen fish followed it to the surface. They'd stayed with us ever since, swimming at a slightly greater depth than the rest and always in a cluster.

But the waters became really crowded when a car-sized cable spool floated by. Had it fallen off a ship in a storm, or was it just another piece of trash dumped into the ocean? We still saw bits of garbage on a regular basis, but this was by far the largest and most unusual. Usually it was a plastic bottle or a jumble of ropes. Sometimes we'd row over to see if anything was growing on it; some garbage is host to barnacles, algae, and even tiny crabs. Colin got quite excited at these moments, and he talked about making "flotsam soup," which I think meant throwing everything edible into a pot. Fortunately, he hadn't done this yet.

We rowed closer to inspect the cable spool, and Colin began talking about the great soup we could make. The spool was covered with the usual algae greens, but we were in for a surprise: underneath the spool was a large group of fish. And they were all keen to jump ship. As we passed the spool, dozens of them glided through the water towards our boat. We saw two types of fish we hadn't seen before, which we nicknamed "floppy fish" and "smarties." The floppy fish, which we later found out were actually triggerfish, were comical in appearance, with oversized dorsal and abdominal fins that wagged like a dog's tail in slow motion. Their mouths were beak-shaped, and they immediately started gnawing barnacles off the bottom of our boat. The smarties were the size of Fred and Ted, but they were a little more rotund and covered in muted polka dots. We called them smarties because we feared that the larger fish would eat them like, well, chocolate Smarties.

While we rowed, the fish stayed by our side, dozens of them frantically swimming beside our boat and under our oars. The smarties, in particular, liked to swim directly under the oars and, on more than one occasion, they got an accidental oar in the face. Each time this happened, the fish that had been hit would be momentarily stunned, like someone who'd absent-mindedly walked into a wall. Then it would give its tail a shake and madly swim to catch up with the group.

Dorado also followed our boat, but more loosely. With their incredible speed, they easily kept pace with us, and they seemed to treat us like a coffee shop—a place to hang out and meet friends. When they first arrived, I worried they would eat Fred, Ted, and the other little ones. Dorado are sleek predators and they swam below most of our fish, almost as if they were sizing them up for dinner. But they weren't. Dorado never chased the small fish that followed our boat. Instead, we watched in amazement as they rocketed after schools of harder-to-catch flying fish, which launched into the skies to escape their predators.

During our first eight weeks at sea, we had caught only one fish—a small dorado near the Canary Islands. Our luck had now changed, and with a growing school of dorado keeping pace with our boat, we caught as many as we needed. In the previous week alone, we had caught eight. This might sound like a lot, but we worried that our stored supplies might not be enough to see us to the other side of the ocean. The bad weather had put us far behind schedule, and we did not know if things would improve. To stretch our provisions, we ate fresh dorado almost daily and even sun-dried several for leaner times. Rather callously, I nicknamed our accompanying school of dorado the "floating larder," the term John Fairfax had given the dorado on his ocean row thirty-five years before.

"I THINK OUR hoochie is getting a little worn," I said, wiggling the hook out of our freshly caught dinner.

"It *has* been getting a lot of action lately," Colin agreed.

The lure had once resembled a green squid, but now it was just a bent, rusty hook with only one of the original eight tentacles remaining. We had only one other lure: a plastic plug shaped like a flying fish. The clerk in the Portuguese sporting goods store had seemed to think it would work well. Hopefully he was right.

We filleted the fish and threw the scraps overboard. Our fish contingent frantically devoured the smorgasbord before it sank. The fish could only descend to about nine metres before they had to abandon their meal and return to the surface. To help them out, we tied a string to the dorado carcass and hung it off the boat. Like chickadees flocking around a suet feeder, or a school of piranhas on a cow, dozens of fish pecked at the carcass. Within a few hours, they'd picked every last bit of meat off the bones, leaving only a skeleton hanging on a string. When we first started feeding the fish like this, I worried we'd also attract sharks, and several mornings we awoke to find the string severed and the skeleton gone. But it was worth the risk.

Fred, Ted, and the other small fish quickly learned the golden dorado was their food source. As time went on, they became emboldened and began attacking the dorado we reeled in with the fishing rod. Occasionally we even noticed them nipping at passing dorado that weren't hooked. Amusingly, the dorado would turn tail—much like a timid German shepherd that has no idea it's twenty times bigger than a yappy Chihuahua.

"DOLPHINS," COLIN SAID excitedly. "Come out here, quick!"

I grabbed the video camera and scrambled onto the deck. The sea exploded with the glistening backs of more than a hundred dolphins heading towards us at breakneck speed. Their pace slowed only when they leapt straight upward, clearing the water by two or more metres and then spinning vertically and plunging back into the sea.

They were spinner dolphins—famous for their acrobatic displays and aptly named for the performances we witnessed. Their habitat is open ocean waters, mostly between the tropics of Cancer and Capricorn, where they travel in groups ranging from several dozen to thousands. At about 175 centimetres long and 50 kilograms, they are smaller than the spotted and bottlenose dolphins in these waters.

"They're so loud," I said with delight.

The air reverberated with high-pitched squeaks and a stream of clicks that sounded like the opening of a super-sized zipper. The dolphins were undoubtedly telling one other that a couple of misplaced humans in a little red boat was blocking their path. Spinner dolphins use squeaks, whistles, and trills for communication. Their rapid-fire clicks, on the other hand, are for echolocation—a type of bio-sonar also used by whales and bats that allows them to locate objects by their echo. In the ocean's turbid waters, this mode of perception is more sensitive than sight.

Their pace towards us continued unabated, and as they neared, several more leapt out of the air in a spinning arc and returned to the sea with a splash. This splash, too, was a form of dialogue. In fact, scientists suspect that spinner dolphins communicate through acrobatic feats, as well. When they leap out of the water and crash down again, the froth of bubbles and loud slap help with both communication and echolocation.

The dolphins surrounded our boat on all sides, and they swam beneath us as well, but they barely paused. Soon, they were out of sight.

"I hope they come back," I said softly, staring into the distance until the last one disappeared.

Just after the sun went down, at least a dozen cetaceans returned, their presence announced by whistles and clicks. It was difficult to see them clearly in the fading light. We could hear them splashing and blowing around the boat for a good twenty minutes. I was thrilled with the wildlife display and gave little thought as to why our boat had suddenly captured the dolphins' attention.

When the sun rose the following morning, I realized the purpose behind their visit: only two dorado remained by our boat, fourteen fewer than yesterday. The dolphins had waited until dark—when fish are practically blind—and then picked them off effortlessly by using their sonar. During the day the dolphins didn't even bother giving chase, knowing the dorado could easily outswim them.

THE WATERS WERE now very calm. At night we slept with the hatch open to let the cooler air into our sweltering cabin. In my journal, I wrote: *All we hear is the roll of the sliding seat and the movement of the water—oars dipping and waves lapping.* Had it not been for contrary currents eroding our progress, it would have been idyllic. But every metre we inched forward, we slipped half a metre back.

However, something beyond adverse currents was worrying me.

"What do you think about starting a family?" I asked.

"We'll have wonderful kids," Colin said, brimming with affection. "We can take them on adventures with us—not things like this—but maybe sailing, or canoeing on the Mississippi River. I've always thought it would be great to . . ."

"Well, actually, I was thinking more immediately," I interrupted.

"You mean, reaching shore with three on board?" Colin asked, his eyes widening.

"My period is four weeks late."

The colour drained from Colin's face. He looked terrified.

"I'm sure it's because of the stress," I quickly continued. "It's just that . . . I've never had this happen before. But I think extreme activity can do that. I've heard this happens to athletes when they're training intensely."

Colin was quiet, his mind running through the possibilities. "So you could be between four and five months pregnant by the time we reach shore, and ready to deliver just as we cycle into Vancouver."

"Yes, that sounds about right."

MY PERIOD WASN'T the only thing late. The day before, we'd spent several hours tapping numbers into our calculator. Our average daily distance since leaving—including *all* the days of contrary weather—had been fifty-two kilometres per day. At this pace it would take us 173 days to cross the Atlantic, more than two months longer than we'd anticipated. Originally, we had optimistically hoped to cross the Atlantic Ocean in 90 days, although we had packed enough food for 130 in case of major delays. With fishing and rationing, we could stretch this supply for another month.

"Our speed will pick up soon, once the remnants of Delta dissipate and the regular winds take hold," Colin said. "If it wasn't for all the storms screwing up the prevailing winds, we'd be more than halfway to Miami by now."

"Thank God hurricane season is finally over," I sighed.

"We should be able to do at least seventy kilometres a day in normal conditions. That would allow us to reach Miami in..." Colin paused as he did the mental calculations. "About seventy days."

I scribbled calculations in my journal, "That's 146 days in total, which makes our arrival date February 14. We'd be on land for Valentine's Day—how romantic!"

"I think we should set a daily distance goal, just like we did when we were cycling," Colin said.

"Seventy kilometres a day it is," I agreed.

Having tangible milestones re-energized our drive—seventy kilometres a day, Miami by mid-February. It transformed the end of the journey from a nebulous goal looming far in the distance to one that inched closer at a measurable rate. The disappointment of storm after storm had created a depressing downward spiral of apathy and frustration. Now, the spark returned. The weather was reasonable, we had set our goals, and we felt ready to charge ahead.

"GUYS, YOU'RE NOT going to believe this," Dean said, the tension in his voice apparent through the satellite phone. "There's another hurricane on the ocean—Hurricane Epsilon."

"I know," I said. "But don't worry, it's not supposed to come anywhere near us."

Colin's mother had told us about Epsilon two days before. It had formed on Colin's birthday right about the time he was blowing out his candles, wishing for no more hurricanes. But it was on the other side of the Atlantic Ocean near Bermuda and was expected to head towards Europe.

"Where is it now?" I asked.

"Well, that's the thing," Dean said. "It started moving northeast, towards Europe, and they thought it would dissipate very quickly. But then yesterday it changed tack and stopped moving north. Since then it's been travelling straight east, and the gap between it and you is closing quickly."

"Good God," I groaned into the handset. "Please tell me I'm having a bad dream."

Colin was looking at me with concern while he rowed.

"Don't worry, guys," Dean continued. "They predict it's going to weaken. By the time it reaches you, it'll be a light breeze."

"Thanks, Dean," I said, grateful for his optimism.

I hung up the phone and relayed the details to Colin.

"Even if it dissipates, it's going to bring contrary winds and currents, and there's no way we'll be able to keep up our seventy kilometres a day in those conditions," Colin said glumly.

Epsilon had developed in the unstable systems left in Delta's wake. It had formed almost three thousand kilometres to our west and was predicted to quickly lose power. Instead, it meandered aimlessly, its track forming a loop, until it strengthened into a hurricane on December 2.

Although hurricane season had officially ended on November 30, Epsilon defied the statistics and even the generally accepted physics of how a hurricane is formed. Conditions for the creation of Epsilon were unfavourable—temperatures were low and wind shear was high. Sea surface temperatures were thought to be only 21 to 24 degrees Celsius, significantly lower than the minimum of 26.5 degrees Celsius required to form a hurricane. Our first hurricane, Vince, had also formed in cool waters, which made us wonder again if something was different about the ocean this year, other than our presence. Were the temperatures actually warmer than hurricane experts thought, or were hurricanes somehow becoming more adept at forming in unfavourable conditions? Epsilon even had the added challenge of extreme vertical wind shear—rapid changes in wind speeds with increasing elevation—which should have negated the rotational forces and made it impossible to become a tropical storm, let alone a hurricane.

After its formation, Hurricane Center forecasters were confident Epsilon would immediately weaken. The day it formed, the advisory stated, "Epsilon should begin to steadily weaken within the next twelve to eighteen hours." Six hours later: "Epsilon has likely reached its peak intensity... and steady weakening should begin within the next twelve to eighteen hours... so the 2005 Atlantic hurricane season can finally end."

But the day after Epsilon reached hurricane status, it showed no sign of weakening and, unfortunately for us, it changed its course. Instead of travelling northeast into the waters of the North Atlantic, where even cooler waters and heightened wind shear awaited, it turned east and headed straight for us. "It appears that Epsilon is running away from the approaching hostile environment," the Center stated. As Epsilon travelled towards us, it gained strength, its wind speeds reaching 142 kilometres an hour. It perplexed the hurricane forecasters, who stated, "Epsilon has continued to strengthen against all odds."

Five days after forming and two days after becoming a hurricane, the exasperation of Hurricane Center forecaster Dr. Lixion Avila was apparent even in the Center's technical updates: "There are no clear reasons, and I am not going to make one up, to explain the recent strengthening of Epsilon." Still, they continued to predict Epsilon would rapidly weaken.

When Dean delivered the news to us, Hurricane Epsilon was in its third day as a full-fledged hurricane, with no signs of slowing. Approximately 1,300 kilometres to our northwest, it was moving eastward at 18 kilometres per hour. Now the storm was predicted to curve to the south, which could put it on a collision course with us.

Dean continued to keep us updated on the hurricane's coordinates, and we plotted its track on our chart. We struggled to figure out the best course of action. We had limited options, but we still had some control over our location. The waters were still calm enough for rowing, and we guessed that we had another twenty-four to forty-eight hours of self-propulsion, potentially moving ourselves a hundred kilometres from our present location. If we knew where the hurricane was going, this distance could make a big difference. But the problem was that we could just as easily row *into* the path of the hurricane as away from it. Where we placed ourselves could mean the difference between life and death, and we struggled to make sense of the forecasts and relevant data.

"I think we should row southward. Look at these storm tracks," Colin said, pointing to a chart with a compilation of hurricane tracks in our *Atlantic Crossing Guide*. "There are fewer late-season storms that track down into lower latitudes."

I looked at the squiggle of lines that crowded the chart. "Hmm, I see what you mean," I said, not entirely convinced.

We were already lower than Miami, and the further south we travelled, the harder it would be to regain the latitude.

"I agree that it wouldn't hurt to reduce our westward progress—maybe we should row southwest instead of due west," I suggested.

Colin agreed that this might help, so we rowed southwest for the rest of the day. Given that a hurricane churned a thousand kilometres away, it was surprising how tranquil the ocean was. Conditions were no longer as calm as they had been just a few days before, but the winds were moderate and the waves were less than two metres. Only an immense, slow-moving swell that raised and lowered our vessel hinted that something was awry. We had a hard time fathoming that northwest of us moved a storm producing two hundred times more energy than the total electrical generating capacity of the world (between 5 and 20×10^{13} watts).

Hurricane Epsilon had been travelling almost due east, and if it continued on this course, it would pass to the north of us. But on December 5, when it was directly eight hundred kilometres to the north, it slowed to a standstill. When it did start moving again, it was at a ninety-degree angle to its previous line of travel, and headed directly towards us.

I couldn't believe it. When we had first heard of Epsilon I had been dismissive. It was on the other side of the Atlantic Ocean, predicted to die within hours, and supposed to head towards Europe. Now the hurricane was continuing to build strength. It was just a few hundred kilometres away and was moving directly towards us at twenty kilometres an hour. This storm was much more powerful than Hurricane Vince, and it would likely be on top of us in forty-eight hours.

"I didn't tell you my birthday wish because I didn't want to jinx it," Colin said as he rowed.

"And what was it?" I said, barely listening as I nailed the interior hatches shut with a small hammer.

"I wished we would have no more hurricanes."

"Yeah, I kind of suspected that was it," I said. "If I were superstitious, I would say that birthday wishes on the ocean are bad luck. It's a good thing you didn't wish good health for all your friends and family."

"It's like flat tires," Colin said.

"What's like flat tires?" I asked.

"The hurricanes," Colin replied, as if it was blatantly obvious. "No one gets as many flats cycling as I do. In Siberia I'd get two or three a day. I've probably averaged at least one a day throughout this expedition. But on the ocean I can't get flats, so the bad luck has to manifest itself in another way."

"Hurricanes," I said. "Of course, why didn't I see the connection? You're a homing beacon for hurricanes and flat tires."

"You have to admit, it's a pretty incredible coincidence," Colin continued. "The worst hurricane season in history, chock-a-block with anomalous hurricanes that all head directly towards us. I mean, Epsilon has had to work hard to persist this long and to get so close to us."

I wondered if I should phone the Hurricane Center and tell them they could stop worrying about predicting hurricanes, because we had it all figured out.

A better-placed phone call would be to my parents. I pulled the satellite phone out of its waterproof case and dialled my mom at her Hamilton apartment.

"Julie, I was waiting for you to call. Are you okay?" she said.

"Yes, Mom, everything is going well," I said.

She didn't know about Epsilon, and since it was highly unlikely she would find out, I didn't tell her.

"On Sunday I went to church and the pastor said he read about you in the paper," my mom said. "He said you saw a big turtle."

Colin had been writing a series in the *Globe and Mail*. I had told my mom about the friendly turtle two weeks before, but I was pleased to revisit the tale and talk of happier times.

"That's right, Mom. It was a big turtle that swam up to us, and we were able to pet him."

"Eek!" she said. "You should be careful, it could bite you."

"No, Mom, it was a friendly turtle."

And so the conversation went. My mom continually worried about me, but her concern was generally off the mark. When I told her we'd had a glass of wine to celebrate Colin's birthday, she became concerned.

"You shouldn't drink wine. Most boat accidents happen when people drink."

My mother's concerns were extensive. Our eating dried dorado spawned concerns over a fish-borne strain of salmonella. She worried we would catch a cold, not eat enough, get our feet wet . . . it was limitless. Nonetheless, I would rather that she fretted about imaginary dangers than the real tempest tearing up the sea only seven hundred kilometres away.

My web-savvy dad, on the other hand, would already know about Epsilon. He'd undoubtedly be monitoring conditions on the Atlantic. After bidding goodbye to my mother, I reached him at his Toronto home.

"Hi, Dad."

"You sound tired."

"No, Dad, I'm fine."

"No, you're not," he said, his deep voice agitated. "Another hurricane is going to hit you."

"No, Dad, we'll be all right," I said, trying to reassure him.

"You've got to get out of there. You're in a part of the ocean that has the greatest room for storms to build—you've passed the point of no return. You have to get to land!"

Get to *land*? Would that be Africa, 3,000 kilometres to our east, or North America, 3,500 kilometres west?

"We can't go to land. We're stuck here in the middle of the ocean in a little rowboat," I said, feeling my cheeks flushing. "There are no other ships in this region; we haven't seen any for days. All we can do is ready ourselves for the hurricane.

We've already battened down the hatches, made the life raft easily accessible, and placed all our emergency equipment at hand. Don't worry, we'll be fine. It's just a hurricane, and we've got a very seaworthy rowboat."

I suddenly realized my last sentence sounded ridiculous and probably didn't reassure my father. Nonetheless, I could do little to offer him comfort. I did my best to explain we were well-prepared and experienced in handling heavy weather. We'd made it through two big storms already—Hurricane Vince and Tropical Storm Delta—and we could make it through one more.

But my father countered my attempts to remain positive by explaining why we wouldn't make it. Our boat was too slow, he said, and even if we did make it through the storm, if we kept up this pace we wouldn't reach Miami until the spring.

After I hung up, I felt even worse than before. I knew he was worried and that I had caused him a lot of grief, but I couldn't help wishing he had have offered a few words of support.

As Epsilon surged towards us, Colin and I spent much of our time reflecting on our lives. In my journal, I wrote: *We contemplate our own mortality as the hurricane north of us decides its course. As the skies darken, and mountainous swells slide down from the north, I wish I were anywhere in the world but here. I fear death, and that terror now permeates every cell in my body. This voyage reinforces the philosophy that life itself is a journey—a journey without a known destination. Even though it is not length that makes it good or memorable, I hope we won't reach our final destination in a few days.*

We continued rowing southwest. The waves had started to crash over the deck, drenching me as I tried to keep the oars steady. Dorado rode the cresting waves as they followed us, seemingly content in the turbulent waters. An enormous school of flying fish took to the air. Dozens of glimmering bodies with fins spread like wings soared above the waves, travelling incredible distances and speeds to escape the predators that chased them below. I found it somehow comforting that for the fish, life went on as normal.

By nightfall, we'd travelled an astonishing fifty-six kilometres. This was excellent speed, considering Epsilon was closing in on us and the weather was degrading quickly. At 9:00 PM, Colin clambered into the cabin. It was my turn to row.

"Maybe we should stop rowing," I said.

Colin stared at the wrinkled chart spread across the bed. I'd just marked our latest position and the coordinates of the hurricane that Dean had relayed an hour earlier. The storm was now 550 kilometres away.

"The Hurricane Center is now forecasting that the storm is going to start travelling southwest. If it does that, we're going to be rowing straight into its course," I said.

Colin shrugged. "They've been wrong about every aspect of this storm. What's to say that it's not going to continue coming straight towards us? At least we'll be moving out of its way then."

We discussed the possibilities for more than an hour before finally deciding the most prudent choice would be to stop rowing. We hoped the latest weather prediction was correct. It would be a stressful night, but we could do nothing more than sit and wait. We lowered the drogue, secured all loose on-deck items, and locked ourselves in the cabin. This routine, unfortunately, was beginning to feel normal.

"It's going to be a rough night," Colin said.

"Sleep tight. I love you," I said.

"I love you, too."

I rolled over onto my side. Just another night in the rowboat.

The breaking waves that smashed into *Ondine* woke me up several times throughout the night, but surprisingly, I got a few hours of sleep. At 6:00 AM my alarm summoned me back to the oars. I clambered out of bed and began putting on my rain gear.

"What are you doing?" Colin asked.

"Getting ready for rowing," I replied.

"We're not rowing. Don't you remember? There's a big hurricane coming our way and we've elected not to row in the hope that this will somehow save our lives," Colin said.

Reality came crashing back into perspective. In my groggy, exhausted state I had blanked the hurricane from my mind and stumbled ahead with the morning routine. The momentary relief of having to climb out into the gale to row was quickly overshadowed by the pending hurricane.

"There should be an updated report on the hurricane," Colin said, glancing at his watch.

He picked up the phone and dialled the number we now knew by memory. I listened carefully to his words, praying for some hint of positive change. Colin suddenly smiled. "Excellent," he said, jotting down some coordinates before turning off the phone.

"Good news," Colin said. "We made the right decision in not rowing. The hurricane has indeed veered to the southwest and is no longer aimed directly for us. At its current direction of heading it should be four to five hundred kilometres to our west. Right now it's only five hundred kilometres away, so things shouldn't get much rougher."

I looked through the Plexiglas hatch out to the grey, windy world. Waves towered around us, their peaks tumbling to create whirlpools of froth. The deck was awash with spray, and waves frequently surged right over it. Nonetheless, our vessel could easily handle these conditions. We had been spared once again.

From the cabin, we continued to monitor Epsilon's progress. It continued moving in a northwest path, and we almost laughed when Dean read us the written reports on the National Hurricane Center's website: "The end is in sight. It really, really is," followed six hours later by "The end is in sight... yes... but not quite yet. I thought I was going to find a weakening system and instead I found that Epsilon is still a hurricane." Finally, on December 8, Hurricane Epsilon weakened enough to lose its hurricane title. It had the distinction of being the twenty-seventh storm of the season, one of only five hurricanes to form in the month of December, and the longest hurricane this month had ever seen. No one could have asked for a more unique birthday present.

Although Epsilon had weakened, the waves were still too big for us to comfortably row, and the currents were not in our favour. We took solace in knowing that the ocean would soon return to a more benign state, and we did our best to power through the waves. We returned to a reduced rowing schedule, rowing only during daylight hours and harnessing ourselves to the boat whenever we were on deck. Finally, two days after Epsilon ceased being a hurricane, the waves stopped crashing over our deck, and we resumed rowing during the night. After more than a week of tumultuous weather, we were finally rowing eighteen hours a day again.

Now, more than ever, we felt that we'd had our fair share of bad weather and that good times lay ahead. Whether that was misplaced optimism I didn't know, but it sure helped keep our spirits up.

12

A BLUE CHRISTMAS

"WHAT ARE THE symptoms of scurvy?" Colin asked. He was massaging his wrist, which had been bothering him for the last few days.

"I think your teeth start falling out, you bleed profusely, and then you die," I said flatly. "I've never heard of sore wrists being attributed to scurvy."

"My gums are feeling a little tender," Colin said, squirming. "How much vitamin C do you need to prevent scurvy?"

I shrugged. Until now I hadn't even considered scurvy as a potential concern. It's not one of those things you think of when planning a first aid kit. We had medication for diarrhea, allergic reactions, and nausea, but somehow, scurvy had slipped under the radar.

"I've read a few stories about sea journeys from the 1500s," Colin continued. "Scurvy decimated their boats—it was the biggest killer. 'Plague,' they used to call it."

I was listening intently. "How long were they out at sea for?"

"A few months, maybe more."

"Hmmm, we've been out at sea for almost three months now. It *has* been a while since we've had any fresh fruits or veggies."

"Do you know if we have any foods with vitamin c?" Colin asked.

I thought for a moment. Citrus fruit would have been ideal, but our bag of lemons had transformed into mouldy balls in the first week.

"The canned vegetables will have some vitamin c, but not as much as fresh ones would. The heat from the cooking and canning process can destroy the vitamin by denaturing it," I said.

"Denature?" Colin asked, looking at me quizzically.

"It just means that the heat breaks down the vitamin c molecule, or changes its form so that it's no longer active."

I pulled back the mattress and opened the hatch that contained our weekly food supply. Crackers, peanut butter, sardines, potatoes, rice, milk—it didn't look promising. Suddenly a little sachet of drink crystals caught my attention. I scanned the nutrition information panel.

"Cplus, fortified with vitamin c," I announced proudly. "But we have enough for only twenty litres."

But Colin wasn't listening to me; he was staring at something in the water. "What about plankton?"

"That's a great idea. Phytoplankton is supposed to be a miracle food—full of vitamin c, fatty acids, minerals, and a bunch of other good stuff."

In Lisbon, a German sailor named Ollie had told us to "get your greens from the sea" as he handed us two pairs of pantyhose. "All you have to do is pull these behind your boat. The fine weave acts like a sieve, and it will strain the plankton right out of the water."

I found the pantyhose in a little-used locker, tied three cords to the waistband, and threw it overboard attached to a thin rope. After a few adjustments, the stockings ballooned open like parachutes. Now all we had to do was row and wait for them to fill with nutritional goodness.

Phytoplankton live in all oceans; they are the building blocks for marine life and create 50 per cent of our oxygen. You can't see these single-celled organisms, but they drift across the oceans (*phyton* is Greek for "plant," and *planktos* means "drifter"). They live in the top layer of the ocean, where sunlight penetrates. Occasionally their density becomes so great that the ocean is discoloured. These algal blooms can even be seen from space, and they're not necessarily a positive phenomenon. In fact, the only algal blooms I have seen were in British Columbia, when "red tide" spread a rusty hue across the water, and phytoplankton released a toxin that made shellfish poisonous. Even though these blooms can be harmful, the survival of most ocean life depends on phytoplankton. They provide food for the smallest fish, which, in turn, sustain the hierarchy of predators above them—all the way up to the largest mammal, the great baleen whale. I just hoped the plankton we brought in would be a healthy addition to our diet.

"This is exciting," Colin said as he rowed with extra vigour. "I've never gone salad-fishing before."

"Hopefully we'll catch a big one."

An hour later I pulled in the stockings.

"Nothing!" I scoffed. "The pantyhose parachute is slowing our speed, and we're not catching anything."

I wasn't sure if the density of plankton was too low, or if the sieve in our stockings wasn't fine enough. Either way, it wasn't working. We decided to give up planning plankton plates, and instead opted to ration our juice crystals for the rest of the voyage. I then remembered the big bottle of multivitamins I'd tossed into the super-sized shopping cart in Lisbon. After an hour of searching, I found it tucked under the spare flares. I ran my finger down the list of supplements. Vitamin c—60 mg. To double-check we phoned Dean's girlfriend, Sarah Evans, who was studying to be a doctor, and she assured us we would not be getting scurvy.

We still weren't sure why Colin's wrist hurt, but it was probably a result of rowing. Rowing is an extremely repetitive sport, especially when you're pulling on the oars for eight or more hours a day. We had already adjusted our rowing technique to minimize this strain, but that probably wasn't enough. The usual rowing technique is to feather the oars—turn the oar blades as the oars leave the water to reduce wind resistance and prevent them from catching water—but we found that repeating that slight twist of the wrist thousands of times a day gave us both tendonitis. Although we had stopped feathering, we suspected it had already done some damage.

WE WERE MAKING better progress now, but the trade winds still hadn't fully recovered from the instability left in Epsilon's wake. They continued to push our boat southward, despite our efforts to regain latitude and to position ourselves for Miami. After several fruitless weeks of struggle, we reassessed our final destination.

"Our efforts to climb northward against these winds are really sapping our westward progress," I said. "Maybe we should consider arriving somewhere south of Miami."

Colin was out on the oars, and our speed was only 0.5 knots. If we angled the boat forty-five degrees to the southwest, our progress would quadruple. I unrolled our chart of the Atlantic Ocean, and we pondered the possibilities. Just south of Miami, the Caribbean Sea presented a labyrinth of reefs and islands that would be dangerous to navigate. The low power of our rowing would leave us at the mercy of the weather, and we didn't want to end the voyage by being blown onto a reef. Much further south, however, the Caribbean Sea was open, with easily navigable waters. If we changed our destination to Costa Rica—2,500 kilometres south of Miami—the elements would be much more in our favour, and the route looked manageable.

In between shifts we looked at the charts together, weighing the pros and cons.

"Let's do it," Colin finally said. "I'm sick and tired of trying to struggle back up to Miami. The most important thing is that we make it across this godforsaken ocean, and undoubtedly our chances of success will be higher if we use the elements to our advantage."

So that was it. On my shift I altered our direction to wsw, towards Limón, Costa Rica, and the boat began moving at 2.5 knots. It would lengthen the distance of our ocean crossing by hundreds of kilometres (as the crow flies, Limón was 1,300 kilometres farther from Lisbon than Miami), and when we reached Costa Rica, we would need to cycle thousands of kilometres farther to get back to Vancouver, but for now, that wasn't important. We just wanted to get across the ocean safely.

A FEW DAYS later, the white sail of a distant boat flickered on the horizon—so small, I could barely see it. Probably a pleasure sailboat heading to the Caribbean islands, I thought. They would not be enjoying these windless conditions. The sea was like a giant lake; not even a ripple marred its glassy surface. The slow swell made the ocean's surface rise and lower like an animal breathing in deep sleep. Although we would have preferred winds in our favour, calm waters were the next best thing, and we were making fine speed.

We were in a celebratory mood, for we had reached the halfway point. We were exactly five thousand kilometres away from Costa Rica. Colin was busy frying pancakes (our party breakfast), and I salivated at the oars as I smelled the golden brown morsels cooking over the alcohol stove. After three months on the ocean, the boat fare was getting quite monotonous, and these pancakes with caramelized sugar would be the treat of the week.

"There's a sailboat in the distance. Would you pass me the VHF radio?" I asked Colin.

The boat was coming in our direction, and I was excited at the prospect of seeing other humans. Since leaving Lisbon, the only people we had talked to face to face were the Spanish fishermen who'd briefly circled our boat. Colin passed me the radio.

I pushed the talk button. "This is rowboat *Ondine* calling unidentified sailboat. Do you copy?"

A male voice answered immediately in clear English. "Yes, we do. We can't see you, though. Where are you?"

"We are at an approximate bearing of 260 degrees from your vessel, perhaps one kilometre away," I replied.

I turned off the VHF radio and squealed in delight. "We're having company!"

I frantically tidied up the boat and put on some clothes. Colin turned off the stove and put breakfast on hold. We watched as the tiny sail in the distance came closer. It was heading too far south, so I radioed to correct their bearing.

"He sounds British, doesn't he?" said Colin.

"Yes," I said, dreamily imagining them handing a big bag of British sweets over the side of the boat.

It took a surprisingly long time for the boat to reach us, and soon I realized why. The boat was much bigger than I had first guessed; it had actually been two or three kilometres away when I'd first spotted it. The thirty-metre luxury sailing yacht finally saw us from about five hundred metres, and it made a final course correction to come alongside. It was powered by a rumbling diesel engine; the mainsail hung listlessly. Its name, *Ripple*, was emblazoned on the hull. The entire crew was on deck as the gleaming white vessel chugged alongside. We felt like a mouse next to an elephant.

"Hello," the captain said in a lilting English accent. A few more hellos and waves followed from the five others on deck, and the captain introduced himself as Alex. "Where are you going?"

"Costa Rica," Colin said.

"How about you?" I asked.

"Antigua. We left the Canary Islands six days ago, and before that we were in the Mediterranean."

I eyed their boat enviously; we had passed through the Canary Islands almost two months before. "When do you think you'll reach Antigua?" I asked.

"It'll be about four or five days. The calm conditions are expected to stay, and we've motored the whole way," Alex said. "We'll give you the recent weather fax. Also, if you want any treats, we've got a galley packed with food."

"Anything you can spare would be great," I said, trying not to scream like a teenager who'd just won a new car on a pop radio station.

"Fran, our chef, will grab a few odds and ends for you."

We chatted animatedly while Fran went inside to collect presents for us. *Ripple* was run by six paid crew members, and the owner, a wealthy businessman, would meet them in the Caribbean. The crew were from a range of countries; most were in their mid-twenties to early thirties. As we stared up from our primitive boat, clad in mildewed clothing and surrounded by chunks of drying dorado meat hanging on strings, I suddenly longed for the decadence and comfort that would come with being on such a luxury boat. Visions of a soft bed, gourmet food, a washing machine, and quick passages filled my mind. And they got paid for it! Suddenly it seemed more ludicrous than ever that we were paying more than fifty thousand dollars to cross the Atlantic in such wretched conditions.

Just then, Fran emerged from the companionway with two bulging shopping bags.

Because of the rolling swell, we kept a distance of about a metre and a half between the boats to prevent them from slamming one another. Colin manoeuvred the *Ondine*'s stern as close to the other boat as he could. Alex used a long boat pole to suspend the bags over the water, and I reached out to retrieve them.

We thanked our new friends profusely, and shortly afterwards they departed with a blast of their horn. In a week they would be swinging in hammocks in Antigua and we—well, we'd still be here.

Excitedly, we emptied the bags.

"Wow—look at this—icy cold beers and pops," Colin exclaimed. "I've been dreaming about cold drinks. I thought it would be another quarter of a year before I'd soothe my chapped lips with a cold one."

"Quick, stick them under the blanket so they hold the cold," I said. "And give me a Heineken while you're at it. Check this bag out—it's full of books and magazines."

Colin suddenly paused.

"Do you remember what your biggest fantasy is—what you've been talking about for the last two months?"

Yes, of course—chocolate. My heart skipped a beat.

"Well, we've got a big box of the finest chocolates in existence," Colin said, as he brought out a large carton of assorted chocolates.

This was definitely the most exciting batch of gifts I had received in my life. We had been out at sea for almost three months. Our food was bland and monotonous, composed of about 40 per cent fish. My thoughts for the past month had revolved non-stop around foods we couldn't have. Suddenly, and completely unexpectedly, we had cold beer, pop, chocolate, candy, cereal, UHT milk, exciting new instant dinners, and a vast array of reading entertainment. Back in the civilized world, this wouldn't have seemed like much, but to me it was a treat like no other.

"What a way to celebrate the halfway point," I said, swigging alternately from a can of Coke and a bottle of Heineken.

We each had another pop, half a can of Pringles, a bag of Doritos, and a few chocolates. The day was hot, and we sat almost immobile as we gorged on these unexpected riches. By day's end we'd drunk six cans of pop each and almost as many beers.

The next day I paid the price for my gluttony. I felt hung over; my head throbbed and a cloud of seediness enveloped me. Colin said it was from all the endorphins released during the previous day's excitement; he felt that way whenever he returned to land after being on sea for a long time.

AS WE CONTINUED sailing towards Costa Rica, the number of dorado swimming under our boat expanded and shrank, depending on the number of dolphins in the region. It seemed that once a dorado joined our boat, it stayed with us until it was eaten by us or, more often, by a dolphin. The school would gradually grow in number as stray fish joined. Often we had more than two dozen dorado swimming with the boat. Invariably, when the school became too big, a pod of dolphins would decimate it in the night, leaving no more than a handful. Each time this happened, we worried that our fish supply might be lost, but then new fish would join the ranks.

Two weeks before, a pair of gigantic dorado had enrolled in our school. They outsized their peers by at least twenty kilograms. They appeared to be male and female (the male has a more bulbous head and is slightly larger). We named the male Legend because "his size is the stuff of legends," as Colin said. We did not want to eat Legend. It seemed a shame to destroy a fish that had survived for so long to reach such magnificent proportions. Plus it would take far too long to process and dry so much meat, and if the weather was wet or rough, it might not dry properly. Instead, we tried to catch Legend's smaller comrades, but avoiding him wasn't easy. The giant fish had reached his grand size by hunting skilfully and by intimidating smaller peers, which also meant he was first to strike at the lure.

We tried to fish only when Legend was off hunting elsewhere; our school of dorado separated into smaller groups to hunt throughout the day. Schools of flying fish broke the surface hundreds of metres in the distance, and our fish streaked just beneath, keeping pace with their airborne prey. After satiating their hunger they came back to our vessel, slowly cruising in the depths below.

Two days before Christmas, we stopped the boat to catch a fish. Legend was off hunting with a few other dorado, and Colin untied the fishing rod. He released about two metres of line and began skipping the flying-fish plug across the water's surface by wagging the tip of the rod back and forth. Without warning, an enormous fish streaked out from under the boat. Before Colin could remove the lure from the water, Legend struck. The rod doubled over and the reel screamed.

"You've caught Legend," I yelled, distraught and full of accusation.

The reel continued to shriek. Legend swam away from us at full speed, but he didn't slow when the line ran out, and it didn't stop him. Instead, the line snapped, and Legend kept on going—free, except with a new piercing adorning his mouth.

"We've lost the lure," Colin said solemnly. "We won't be eating dorado anymore."

I didn't say anything; it was just too sad. Without fish, we were back to stew and rice, canned tuna, and dried bread.

Legend leapt into the air, madly shaking his body in an attempt to rid himself of the lure we so desperately wanted.

"We could try to catch Legend with the old hoochie," Colin suggested.

I thought about it for a moment. The old lure had a rusty hook that was on the verge of breaking, and the plastic squid that concealed the hook had been chewed to almost nothing. I couldn't imagine even the most desperate fish going for it, let alone one enraged at having a hook in its mouth. And if, miraculously, Legend did bite, we could take bets on what would snap first—the hook or the line.

"That's a great idea," I said, with more than a hint of sarcasm. "Let's try catching the huge fish that broke our line with the last remnants of fishing gear we have."

Colin either missed my sarcasm, or refused to acknowledge it. He tied the hoochie onto the line and started fishing. But Legend didn't approach the boat. He stayed at least fifty metres away, repeatedly jumping, the plastic and metal lure clinking as he shook frantically. Although Legend ignored us, I was wrong about the lure having no appeal. Seconds after the lure touched the water, a dorado was hooked.

"We can try again and use this fish for bait to catch Legend," Colin said.

Miraculously, the hook held, and Colin played the fish in. He cut it open, and we were shocked at the small metal object that fell out.

"Is that the weight?" I asked in awe.

Colin picked it up and laughed. "I don't believe it," he said. "When the line broke, the lead weight slipped off it, and this fish ate it. What are the chances?"

The odds of that happening did indeed seem minuscule, but that we would then catch the lead-munching fish out of the dozen that surrounded our boat was even more improbable. Maybe this was a lucky sign. Maybe Legend would bite our hook next, and then we'd have both our weight and lure.

But Legend didn't bite. We used a long, thin strip of fish as bait, and the dorado chased it—all except for Legend. It was a struggle not to catch the other fish, a sort of game in which we lifted the lure into the air when they came too close. Legend was still close by and sporadically leapt into the air trying to shake his piercing, but he had no interest in us. After almost an hour, we gave up. Colin put the fishing rod away, and I started rowing.

Then, suddenly, Legend executed a particularly vigorous jump. He reached a height of several feet, and his body snapped back and forth trying to shake the lure. The setting sun reflected off his wet, golden body, emitting strobe-like flashes. Suddenly a small object sailed through the air. It took a moment for me to register what was happening.

"Colin," I screamed, "Legend's shaken the lure. It's over there!" I pointed to the water sixty metres away.

Without a moment's hesitation, Colin jumped in and swam towards it. I prayed that no sharks would notice we'd just rinsed fish blood and guts into this water, and that the lure wouldn't sink.

"I've got it," he yelled, holding the lure high above his head like the greatest trophy in the world. "I've got it."

CHRISTMAS MORNING STARTED with UHT milk and corn flakes—a breakfast we'd been awaiting since Santa Claus (aka *Ripple*) dropped by a few days before and given us these treats. It was the best bowl of cereal I'd ever had. We decorated the boat with gold foil stars and sang Christmas carols throughout the day.

I have always loved Christmas, and I was determined to make the most out of this one. When I was young, Christmas was a holiday my Christian mom celebrated and even my Muslim dad seemed to enjoy. We decorated our artificial tree, and my mom baked delicious gingerbread cookies and almond crescents. One Christmas Eve my dad played a cassette of Santa noises after I had gone to bed. I lay under the covers hearing Santa laugh and shuffle around the house, deciding where to place the presents. (I was tempted to climb out of bed and find him, but I was scared this might be construed as naughty and that my presents would be withheld.)

I spent some of my favourite Christmases in Meppen, Germany, with my relatives. My mother and I lived with my grandparents and uncle for a year and a half before I started grade school, and we returned every summer during my school years and a few times in the winter. Germany was my favourite place when I was growing up. It was a constant that never changed while we moved from city to city, a place where I was surrounded by family—Oma, Opa, aunts, uncles, and the family dog Buffy. My grandfather taught me the alphabet and had a backyard with fruit trees. It was a fun, carefree place.

In comparison, life in Canada was tumultuous. We moved a lot because of my father's job with the military. My parents also had a rocky relationship. Things did not improve after they divorced and I entered my rebellious teenage years.

We had just moved from Edmonton to Trenton, and the combination of living in a new city and a new family structure may have made things even more difficult. I had always been painfully shy, and I wished that I was more extroverted. Some of my shyness stemmed from being an only child with very strict parents. My father's half-serious threats of shipping me off to a Syrian boarding school or marrying me off to a Middle Eastern man in exchange for an olive farm were very effective at keeping me in line. But with my father absent, I grew bolder, and my mother struggled not only with her new situation, but with her suddenly headstrong daughter.

Life in our home became a constant conflict. I desperately wanted to finish high school so that I could leave for university, but that was still two years away. Eventually I realized I couldn't wait that long. At sixteen I moved out, and finished my grade 12 year while working as a waitress in a mediocre restaurant and a cook at a pizza parlour. Distance improved my relationship with my mother, and I returned home to complete grade 13. The following year, I started my Bachelor of Science at McMaster University in Hamilton, Ontario.

This Christmas was one of the few I would not be home with my mother. Instead, we held our celebrations by satellite phone. Colin also phoned his mother, and we called a few of our closest friends as well. Dean had sent out our Christmas wishes by e-mail to all those who followed our journey, and when we called him on Christmas Day, he read out letters that people had sent us. Colin and I shared the earpiece so that we could both hear. Dozens of people from all across Canada and from as far away as Russia had sent their best wishes. The inspiring and sometimes humorous messages made us feel privileged to have such a wonderful group of supporters. I felt more enthusiastic than ever to row the rest of the way across the Atlantic.

For Christmas dinner we wanted to catch a fish, but the dorado numbers around our boat were rather low due to a recent dolphin visit. Legend was one of the few dorado that had survived the slaughter. As soon as Legend was out of sight, Colin dropped the lure into the water and began rhythmically jerking it back and forth. Ted, Fred, and the other small fish gathered around the lure, but no dorado. Then, with a golden flash, Legend lunged at the lure and bit. The line screamed—it was happening all over again.

But this time the line didn't part; Legend slowed down and fought with less vigour than a fish half his size. Colin reeled him in slowly until he was next to our boat.

"Don't worry, Legend," I murmured. "We won't hurt you."

I gently wrapped my hands around his body to steady him while Colin removed the hook. Legend's body pulsed in my hand, but he remained completely calm. It was as if he knew this would be easier than the previous ordeal of struggling to free the hook. Colin worked the hook out, and we set Legend free.

There was no fresh fish for Christmas dinner; we dined on risotto with canned tuna and corn, followed by canned pineapple for desert. It was a stark contrast to the traditional turkey, stuffing, and cranberry sauce, but I couldn't dream of a better way to celebrate the holidays. We toasted with glasses of Portuguese ice wine and sang Christmas carols. Meanwhile, Legend dashed through the waves, catching flying fish for his own dinner.

13

ONE HUNDRED DAYS
AT SEA

"A HUNDRED DAYS AT sea," Colin said. "Can you believe you've been in this boat that long?"

No, I couldn't. It was incredible. Before leaving I'd had so many doubts about my own abilities. Would I be able to cope with the solitude, seasickness, and physical difficulties? Would an injury do me in, forcing us to abandon the journey? Most of all, I wondered what it would be like to endure so many months of isolation. But here we were, still moving forward.

We had survived two hurricanes and a tropical storm, a near freighter collision, and an overly friendly fishing boat with poor spatial judgement. We were long past the halfway mark, slowly closing the gap between us and North America. I felt on top of the world, and all doubts about my abilities had long vanished. I knew I would be able to complete this journey. In the last hundred days, I had learned an important lesson. It wasn't a huge revelation or the unveiling of a closely guarded secret; it was a simple message I had heard many times from different voices. John Ridgway had said it when I bought the boat, and Colin lived by it: never give up. Even when life looks its bleakest, keep trudging forward, and eventually things will improve. The bulldozer blade of time will push you forward, and the tough times will become distant memories—stories to tell friends and learning experiences that make you appreciate life's comforts all that much more.

NEW YEAR'S EVE came and went with little fanfare. We opened the last two beers that the yacht *Ripple* had given us, and toasted the fish who lazily swam beneath our temporarily free-drifting vessel. We had no New Year's resolutions, just hopes that the good winds would continue.

"Do you know what the world's longest rivers are?" Colin asked.

His intent with this question seemed to have more to do with filling the silence than with sharing useful information—a bit like the games of "I Spy" we played while rowing. Besides, he had already quizzed me on this geographic factoid a few weeks before.

"Nile, Amazon, Yangtze, Mississippi, and Yenisey," I answered.

"Right," Colin said, seemingly delighted with my response. "Unless you think of the ocean currents as rivers. Right now we're on a big river."

"Well, I wish it would flow a little faster."

Countless rivers and streams transport salt water from the Pacific to the Atlantic, from the Northern Hemisphere to the Southern, from the surface to the depths in a never-ending circulatory system. We were on the equatorial currents, powered by the trade winds, which flow westward across the Atlantic between the tropics of Cancer and Capricorn.

The trade wind currents have flowed for a very long time. They received their name from seventeenth-century traders who relied on the winds to transport goods by ship. But that doesn't mean they'll always be here. We found the trade winds and currents far less pronounced than our reference books and charts suggested they would be, and we were not alone in noting the discrepancies. Researchers discovered that both the Pacific trade winds and the thermohaline currents—the latter often referred to as the Great Ocean Conveyor Belt because they flow at a greater depth—have slowed. The cause? Global warming, which decreases ocean salinity by melting Arctic ice, which in turn affects the density-driven thermohaline currents and alters wind patterns by increasing evaporation-impacted trade winds.

Changing currents and winds were an inconvenience not only for us. Sea turtles depend on winds and currents for migratory routes, and Europeans rely on them for a mild climate. Some scientists have predicted that if the Gulf Stream, which is dependent on thermohaline currents, were to stop, Europe would be plunged into a miniature ice age. This would make La Coruña, Spain, feel more like Halifax, Nova Scotia. Both cities are situated at approximately the same latitude; the marked difference in temperature (average January temperature in Halifax is minus five degrees Celsius, while La Coruña is ten degrees Celsius) is because La Coruña is warmed by the Gulf Stream, and Halifax is cooled by the south-flowing Labrador Current.

The last major changes in ocean currents occurred 55 million years ago, when the world's temperatures spiked. Major currents shut down, and others caused widespread mortality of sea life. Changes in ocean currents may have contributed to even higher temperatures by thawing frozen methane deposits at the bottom of the sea, which then bubbled to the surface, reacted with oxygen, and created carbon dioxide.

A quick glance at the GPS told me the currents were still slack. Even though we were in an equatorial zone where the trade winds blew, the wind was variable and the currents paltry. Ocean abnormalities were starting to feel common, and once again, I felt as though we were experiencing changes caused by global warming firsthand.

WHILE I WAS at the oars on January 5, I noticed something fluttering down from the heavens like a discarded receipt. As it drew closer, I realized it was a butterfly, quite large and roughly resembling a monarch in coloration. The butterfly circled our boat for less than a minute, briefly landed on my hand, and then continued across the sea.

We puzzled over the existence of a butterfly that must have flown at least four thousand kilometres across the ocean without food. The insect had probably begun its flight in Africa and had been carried aloft by a storm, then transported by brisk winds high in the troposphere. Interestingly, we had only seen flying insects on three previous occasions, and each time was before a major storm.

In the days leading up to Hurricane Vince, we had seen insects for the first time, and we'd puzzled over their origin. At the time, we were only three hundred kilometres from Africa, but that still seemed a long distance for an insect to fly. We wondered if they'd come from another ship, but the ocean was relatively empty, so that, too, seemed unlikely.

Then, a month later, just a few days before Tropical Storm
Delta had arrived, a small white moth had flown past our
boat. Then thousands of kilometres from the nearest land,
we were even more perplexed. The third sighting occurred
in the days preceding Hurricane Epsilon, when what looked
like a housefly briefly hovered near our boat.

The coincidence just seemed too uncanny. Somehow,
flying bugs on the ocean and hurricanes had to be related. A
wave of low pressure that emanates from Africa and sweeps
across the ocean often precedes hurricanes and tropical
storms. We guessed this had something to do with it. Perhaps unwilling, light, airbound travellers were caught up in
that wave, blown great distances, and then scattered across
the ocean.

If not for our satellite telephone, our recent visitor would
have been cause for uncertainty and speculation. But thanks
to modern technology, we didn't have to speculate; we could
find out for sure if another storm was on the way. On the
first day of 2006, we'd wondered why the long-awaited trade
winds didn't materialize. That's when we'd found out that,
against all odds, a tropical storm had formed 1,500 kilometres northeast of us on December 30. At the time, the storm
was still far enough away that we didn't worry, but now a
quick phone call to Dean confirmed it was moving closer.

Tropical Storm Zeta formed more than four weeks after
hurricane season officially ended, catching the National Hurricane Center off guard and going unnoticed until after it
became cyclonic. Later, on the National Hurricane Center's
website, we read some of the discussion on Zeta and laughed
at one forecaster's wisecrack: "The atmosphere seems to want
to develop tropical storms ad nauseam." Who could blame

them for their somewhat curmudgeonly response—these guys were overworked. I, for one, would have used much stronger language—which I did; thankfully, no one but Colin was there to hear it.

Zeta formed 1,200 kilometres northwest of the Cape Verde islands and began moving west—towards us, of course. Just like Epsilon, it was consistently predicted to diminish, but unfortunately, Zeta also shared its predecessor's resilience and defied all predictions to persist for nine days.

As Zeta approached, eerie conditions blanketed the sea. Cirrus clouds streaked the sky, the winds stopped, and the sea calmed, except for an enormous swell hinting of distant chaos.

We went through our very well-rehearsed routine of preparing for the storm and plotting the cyclone's movement. As gale-force winds drove three-storey waves into our boat, we cocooned in the cabin. The centre of the storm was a mere five hundred kilometres away—uncomfortably close.

Not surprisingly, by this time we were terribly sick of hurricanes, tropical storms, contrary currents, and dysfunctional winds. The tremendous fear we'd experienced at our first hurricane was still there, but it had been dulled. We felt reasonably confident that we would survive, but we knew how much discomfort we would soon be in and that the storm would delay us at least several days.

Just as we had with Vince, Delta, and Epsilon, we spent the worst of the weather lying in the cabin wishing we were elsewhere. We dreamed about living on Vancouver Island and growing a vegetable garden. Our makeshift drogue still trailed in the water, and occasionally we went out to check that it was still there. Waves broke over our boat; with our bilge pump, we removed the water that collected in the cockpit. We ate crackers and cookies and obsessively peered out the window hatches looking for shipping and diminished waves. When conditions improved slightly, Colin tried rowing, but he gave up after a series of waves knocked him off his seat and almost broke the oars. Instead we took turns sitting in the rowing seat, steering the boat with the rudder to keep it from broaching. We tied ourselves to the boat to prevent being washed overboard, but the waves still sluiced over us, often with sufficient force to knock us onto the deck.

Eventually Zeta quieted enough for us to resume rowing, and by the time the storm finally dissipated on January 9, we were rowing full days again. We breathed a sigh of relief when the National Hurricane Center once again bid farewell to the 2005 hurricane season. The official discussion for Tropical Storm Zeta ended with these parting words: "I suppose it is only fitting that the record-breaking 2005 Atlantic hurricane season ends with a record-breaking storm. Today Zeta surpassed 1954 Alice #2 as the longest-lived tropical cyclone to form in December and cross over into the next year. Zeta was also the longest-lived January tropical cyclone. In addition, Zeta resulted in the 2005 season having the largest accumulated cyclone energy, or ACE, surpassing the 1950 season. So, until the 2006 season begins, unless Zeta somehow makes an unlikely miracle comeback, this is the National Hurricane Center signing off for 2005 . . . finally."

All in all, it had been an unbelievable year for hurricanes and tropical storms, and once again, I hoped this would be the end of it.

14

MAGNIFICENT FRIGATEBIRDS
AND FLYING FISH

As we continued rowing towards Costa Rica, the sky
and sea began to look more benign. Small white
clouds dotted the sky, and light winds blew from the
east. Occasionally, waves broke against our boat, but rarely
with enough force to soak me and even when they did, it felt
pleasant, like a refreshing break on a hot day. I washed my
hair and Colin detangled my one obscene dreadlock, which
had formed during Zeta's visit. I did the same for him. Each
day we went swimming, taking turns jumping overboard for
a quick dip while the other stood on shark watch. Fred and
Ted still swam with us, as did a handful of dorado and a col-
lection of smaller fish. Whenever we dove in, Fred and Ted
and the other smaller fish made a beeline towards us, but
scattered when they realized we were not edible.

"Julie, there are insects out here," Colin yelled one sunny
day.

"Oh, no," I groaned. Did this mean another tropical storm?

"No, these are different. They're sea skaters."

I looked outside to find dozens of tiny sculling insects on the water's surface. They walked on water, just like the striders I used to see on the surfaces of lakes and ponds. Their light weight, distributed across six long legs, helps them use the water's surface tension to stay afloat, and the hydrophobic hairs on their legs repel water. But what we found most interesting was how they moved *across* the water's surface. They row. Their two middle legs act like a sculler's oars, while their front and back legs remain stationary, helping with balance and direction. Although I couldn't actually see them rowing—these sea skaters were too small—I quite liked the idea of being surrounded by other rowers.

Plus, they were a fun distraction from the growing discomfort in my hands. Every night, my hands swelled and became like claws, and each morning I uncurled my fat fingers one by one. After a few minutes of rubbing and stretching, they straightened enough to be of use, but they still hurt and seemed to be aching more than usual.

Finally I confided my worries to Colin.

"I think I'm getting arthritis," I said.

"What makes you say that?" Colin asked.

"Look at my hands," I said. "I can't straighten my fingers. They're swollen and they hurt."

Colin looked at my hands closely. "Does anyone in your family have arthritis?"

"Yes," I said with dismay. "My mom, my aunt, my grandmother when she was alive . . . Hmmm, I'm not sure about my dad's family . . ."

"I don't think you have anything to worry about. I think it's just your ligaments thickening. I had the same thing happen to me when I was tree-planting."

Colin's hands looked fine now—apparently holding a shovel all day was harder on his digits than rowing—and he didn't even wear gloves to protect his fingers like I did. My hands looked like they belonged to an eighty-year-old construction worker. Thick calluses, which had thankfully replaced earlier painful blisters, caked my palms, while my fingers had become plump sausages. My engagement ring was a tourniquet that I'd spent hours struggling to remove a month before.

Besides plump fingers, sunburns, salt sores, and the occasional unidentifiable ache, we were actually doing quite well. But this didn't stop me from worrying, and Colin wasn't much better. Minor pains in our sides became appendicitis; extended headaches became brain tumours. So many serious things could have gone wrong—broken bones, botulism, infections, dental mishaps—and since the nearest medical help was an ocean away, fretting about our health was easy. Invariably, however, the pain would dissipate, and then the "life-threatening" condition would be forgotten.

My menstrual cycle was still on hiatus, but I was now sure it was due to ongoing physical stress. With no morning sickness, swollen or tender breasts, or cravings for olives, I felt confident we'd reach shore as a party of two. Still, a pee-on-a-strip test would have been nice.

Our suboptimal nutrition became a growing concern as the months ticked by. A friend of mine, Christine Leakey, sought advice for me from the nutritional company she worked for, Truestar Health. Their CEO, Tim Mulcahy, became intrigued by our trip. He realized we would benefit from their nutritional supplements, and that's how Truestar Health joined our expedition as lead sponsor. They designed a health care plan for us and arranged to deliver the vitamins and supplements. Since we had changed our course to Limón, Costa Rica, we would travel through the Caribbean Islands, making it possible for a boat from the islands to meet us or for us to go ashore.

This new development, which transpired within the digital corridors of our satellite communications equipment, was reason to celebrate. We could now look forward to improved health and an easing of our financial crisis. We toasted our new partnership with Truestar Health with cups of Cplus drink and American cookies.

The Caribbean islands were still a thousand kilometres away, but I was enraptured by the prospect of stopping and visiting one of these tropical jewels. Colin, on the other hand, felt such a visit was too risky and would jeopardize our vessel. Although I knew making landfall in such a low-powered boat held risks, I felt these could be negated if we watched the weather closely and adjusted our course correspondingly. We discussed the pros and cons of making an island landing, and finally decided to stop at the island of St. Lucia. There we could not only meet with Truestar, but re-provision and experience the idyllic bliss of an island oasis. Equally important, we could pick up large-scale charts for the trip to Costa Rica. We had charts for Miami, but not for Costa Rica, and we reasoned that having proper charts for the journey ahead would make up for the risks associated with landing on St. Lucia.

As I daydreamed about margaritas and fruit salad, a huge bird unlike any we had seen before began circling our boat. It was completely black, except for a red sack hanging from its neck, with a forked tail and enormous pointed, bat-like wings. It stayed high in the air, effortlessly propelling itself not with the subtle gliding movement of shearwaters, but with the dramatic soaring movement of eagles, hawks, and other great birds of prey.

"Colin, come see this bird," I yelled.

Colin came out of the cabin just in time to see it plummet in a spiralling descent. With its highly acute vision, the bird had spotted a fish or small turtle from hundreds of metres away, and was going in for the kill. I nervously peered into the waters surrounding our boat, looking for Fred, Ted, and friends. They were no match for this ferocious predator, and I hoped they'd stay close to the boat. The bird soared back to the skies and continued its hunt for food.

"Wow," Colin said with a low whistle. "That is one acrobatic bird. What do you think it is?"

"I don't know. I've never seen a bird like that. The red sack reminds me of a turkey vulture, but the wings are so unusual."

Colin flipped through the pages of our guidebook and, after a few minutes, he announced, "It's a magnificent frigatebird, also known as a man o'war or pirate bird because it attacks other birds and steals their food." Colin went on to explain that the magnificent frigatebird's wingspan can reach two and a half metres, and that they are the lightest birds in the world—meaning that they have the longest wingspan-to-body-weight ratio. Essentially they are airbound; they can't walk well, but can stay aloft for over a week.

"I think it must have come from the Caribbean islands," I said. "Given that they live on the open ocean, I wonder why we haven't seen any before." I'd first assumed seeing this bird meant we were close to land and was mildly disappointed to learn otherwise.

"You're partially right," Colin said. "They do breed in the Caribbean islands, as well as Florida and the Cape Verde islands. But they're tropical birds, and I guess until now, our latitude has been too northerly. But maybe this guy has a nest in the Caribbean; it says here they feed their chicks until they're one year old. Oh, wait. It's only the female that feeds her chicks that long. The male ducks out after three months and tries to find another breeding female."

"Men."

"And that was a male we saw—you can tell by the red throat pouch, which puffs up like a balloon during mating season. Females don't have that, and they also have a white patch on their bellies."

Two shearwaters now joined the magnificent frigate-bird in the skies overhead, each occasionally diving into the ocean to grab a small fish or shrimp. But the frigatebird soon overshadowed the shearwaters' success. It turned its attention from the fish in the ocean to that in the smaller bird's possession. With a few deft aerial movements, the frigatebird asserted its dominance and, when the shearwater dropped its catch, the frigatebird quickly claimed it. So that's how it had earned its warring nicknames.

Our boat had long been a magnet for birds, almost certainly because of the fish following our boat. The birds seemed to have no interest in the smaller pilot fish and trig-gerfish; only the larger dorado captured their attentions. The frigatebirds would follow the dorado, observing their actions from above. When the dorado gave chase to a school of flying fish, the birds spiralled down to the ocean's surface and raced after the airborne dorado. I was amazed to see these birds with almost three-metre wingspans perform such elaborate aerobatics. At the same time, I couldn't help but feel sympathy for the flying fish, which had spent millions of years developing a unique defence mechanism to escape from underwater predators, only to be picked off by these miniature fighter jets.

When chased, flying fish race through the water at top speed before launching into the air, giving the water a final flick with their forked tails to increase their velocity. The timing of the final flick is an important part of the process. In the instant when most of its body is in the air (where resistance is negligible) and its tail pushes off the water, the flying fish doubles its speed to approximately sixty kilometres an hour, allowing it to glide thirty to forty metres.

We saw some flying fish extend their glide without fully re-entering the water. As they arced downward near what I thought was the end of their flight, they dipped their tails into the water and vigorously propelled themselves back to gliding speed. A few times we saw them stay above the ocean's surface for two hundred to four hundred metres, with nothing more than an occasional tail-dip to maintain forward speed.

On his previous journeys, Colin had had flying fish accidentally hit the sail of his old boat during the night. (During the day, they would see the boat and take evasive measures, but their eyesight failed them in the dark.) After they fell into the boat, he had no choice but to pan-fry them for breakfast. Unfortunately, the only flying fish that landed on our vessel were less than three inches long; the larger ones had sufficient power to clear our decks.

Only one irregular object obstructed fish flight path over our boat: Colin or me at the oars. Colin had been hit twice and I'd been smacked once, but we never managed to capture the culprits before they slipped back to the sea through the scuppers. The collisions always happened at night, when our imaginations worked overtime and the ocean already seemed alive with unknown monsters. Colin was hit first, and he screamed like a B-grade actress in a horror movie, thinking the meaty hand of Davy Jones had whacked him on the back of the neck. Soon after, Colin had his turn to laugh at me. It's rather surprising how much punch a trout-sized fish can pack when it's hurtling through the air at sixty kilometres an hour.

"I THINK WE should have gotten more cans of beans and fruit salad, and less dried bread," I said, looking into the bow storage compartment with dismay. It was the morning of day 112; we still had dozens of packages of Melba-toast-like bread, but little else. We had grown sick of the dry bread, especially without butter or cheese to liven it up.

"Have no worries. I've dreamed up a recipe that'll transform those wretched biscuits into something fit for a princess," Colin said.

"Mmm, I can't wait."

We had been trying innovative recipes to make use of the dried toast, but with limited success. So far we'd discovered pan-fried stuffing (dried bread moistened in water, mixed with a can of beans, and fried in oil), bread pudding (milk boiled with bread), and croquettes (moistened bread mixed with canned tuna and sculpted into patties that we pan-fried).

Since we had to ration our flour, we also crushed bread and used it to coat our fish before pan-frying.

I looked away while Colin prepared breakfast so that I didn't ruin the surprise. Finally Colin rang the breakfast bell, vigorously banging a pot with a spoon. He handed me a towering plate of pancakes.

"Can you guess what's special about these?" he asked.

I chewed thoughtfully. "Mmmm, these taste even better than usual—they're lighter and fluffier."

Colin looked pleased with himself. "They're 80 per cent crushed bread! I mixed a little bit of flour with milk powder, water, baking powder, sugar, and a lot of crushed bread. And the syrup, of course, is the usual caramelized sugar with a bit of water."

"I think you've got something here! They're much lighter than normal, and the bread adds a rich flavour, but you'd never know what it is. If people knew how good these were, upscale restaurants around the world would start serving 'rowboat pancakes.'"

Necessity is the mother of invention, and between dried bread and fish from the ocean, we could feasibly make it all the way to Costa Rica. I hoped, however, that conditions would be right for a Caribbean landing, and that we would spend our final month at sea eating a more varied diet. We were now 160 kilometres from the island of St. Lucia, and my excitement at seeing land in a couple of days—and possibly even stepping onto it—was overwhelming. We had been on the water for almost four months, and I longed to be anywhere but this rowboat.

15

A CARIBBEAN PARADISE
IN ST. LUCIA

"WAKE UP," COLIN yelled from outside.

It was still dark, and a glance at the luminous dial on my watch informed me it was only 5:00 AM. We had been rowing non-stop throughout the night in order to stay on course and make landfall on St. Lucia later that day.

"I'm coming," I said.

I pulled on my windbreaker and rowing gloves and peered through the hatch into the dark sea. Although I could barely make out the waves, a cacophony told me the wind was strong and the waves big. Colin's body gyrated on the rowing seat as he struggled to control the boat.

As I opened the hatch to climb out of the cabin, Colin screamed, "Hatch!"

I instinctively pulled it closed and secured it. The roar of an enormous wave reverberated through the cabin, and the boat rolled onto its side. I lost my balance and slammed against the wall. Pencils, books, and cookie packages tumbled on top of me. The boat teetered on its side, on the verge of capsizing, before it righted itself.

I looked outside to where Colin should have been, but he was gone.

"*Colin!*" I screamed as I yanked open the hatch and scrambled outside.

Please be okay, please still be on the boat, I prayed. My mind conjured a horrific scene: a bare boat and an empty, black, pitching sea. This couldn't happen now. We'd been through so much, and land was only hours away.

I couldn't see him. But I heard him yell: "I'm fine."

I followed his voice to see him lying on the deck. The wave had thrown him off the rowing seat; he had not gone overboard.

"Holy shit... that was one mother of a wave! It just reared up out of nowhere. I grabbed onto the safety line to keep from going overboard. Unfortunately, the boat rolled into the oar and snapped it."

I shook with relief. "Thank God you're all right. I didn't see you right away, and I thought maybe..."

"It's okay," Colin said, wrapping his arms around me. I hugged him tightly and held back the hot tears that welled in my eyes. The malevolent black sea crashed around us, and suddenly I felt we had landed on the set of a Harlequin Romance movie directed by Stephen King. The broken oar hung from the oarlock like a severed limb. Its lower half, still attached by a few strands of carbon fibre, knocked against the hull.

After a long minute, I reluctantly released Colin from my grip.

"I can't believe we broke an oar," I said.

"I know. We've been through two hurricanes and two trop-ical storms without incident, and now, as we get near land, it finally snaps."

There was actually a simple reason why the oars had never broken up until now. Normally we stopped rowing when the winds rose above forty knots, securely lashing the oars inboard, where they were protected. At this point the wind was blowing at about forty-five knots, and the waves were very powerful, but we couldn't afford to stop rowing. The ele-ments drove us towards the eastern side of St. Lucia, where the swell crashed into the cliffs and sent plumes of foaming water hundreds of feet into the air. We would probably not survive being wrecked against the cliffs.

We had to row non-stop to fight our way northward so that we could clear the top end of the island before slipping into the lee of St. Lucia. I quickly unlashed one of our spare oars to replace the broken one.

"Good luck," Colin said, just before he retreated into the cabin. "Oh yeah, I almost forgot to tell you: take a look over there."

He pointed westward, and suddenly I noticed the twinkle of lights.

"Oh my God, it's land!" I screamed.

It was surreal. We'd been on the boat for what seemed an eternity, and finally I was looking at solid land again. I couldn't wait to get off this stormy ocean and finally set my toes on solid ground.

"Happy rowing," Colin said.

He closed the hatch firmly in case we capsized, and I felt all alone on the rough sea. Twilight set in, and I watched in awe as the shadowy folds of St. Lucia became discernable. The jagged island was composed of several towering volcanic peaks, their summits obscured within clouds. Lush green slopes cascaded down to the ocean's edge, hinting at the abundant rainfall in this region. We were still twenty kilometres away, but I could already see plumes of white foam against the sheer cliffs that ran along the western flanks of the island. I had barely slept in the past thirty-six hours; I felt like I was dreaming. As huge waves buffeted and twisted our vessel, I felt terrified; at the same time, I couldn't believe that thatched huts, sandy beaches, and gourmet restaurants were so close by. But the ocean's ferocity prevented me from feeling relief. I struggled at the oars, and the imposing cliffs in the distance seemed all too close.

Colin emerged at 7:00 AM and spent several minutes studying the outline of St. Lucia and glancing at the GPS plotter.

"If we want to reach land, we'll have to stay very close to the tip of the island," he said. "Otherwise the current will carry us past the islands, and we won't be able to row back against the winds. We have almost no margin of error. If we're too far south, we'll be driven into the cliffs; too far north, and we'll be blown right past St. Lucia. The current and winds are pushing us forward at almost two knots, so we want to be careful."

The conditions gave us very little control of our direction. We were on a giant westward-moving conveyer belt and could only alter our heading by about twenty degrees north or south. We had to row almost due north to achieve a WNW heading, which meant we were rowing sideways to the waves, placing the boat in a very vulnerable position.

As the island drew nearer, Colin suddenly reversed direction and began rowing towards the cliffs. I shivered as I watched nine-metre swells release the energy they'd gathered across the Atlantic in one final, explosive display.

Pensive, I watched the cliffs become nearer and nearer. "Don't you think it's time we changed our course?" I finally said.

But Colin was distracted by something in the distance, and didn't respond. Then I saw what held his attention: a boat! An open fibreglass fishing boat powered by an outboard motor headed towards us.

"*Bonjour!*" yelled one of the three men onboard.

"*Bonjour!*" I yelled back. I guessed they were from Martinique, a neighbouring French island north of St. Lucia.

"*Habitez-vous Martinique?*" I yelled in my rusty high-school French.

"*Oui!*" the man replied.

I felt thrilled to talk to other humans face to face, but these fishermen had little interest in us.

One of the men pointed beneath our boat. "*Poisson?*"

I nodded my head. They dropped their baited lines into the water and made a wide circle around our boat, moving at about six knots.

I peered into the water. Ted, Fred, and crew had followed us all the way here. Thankfully the fishermen wouldn't be interested in such small fish. They wanted dorado. As these men surely knew, schools of dorado gather under flotsam and other slow-moving objects. I searched the waters beneath us, but couldn't see any of our golden friends. Perhaps they were off hunting or had been scared away by the noise of the motor.

But then it began. The lines jerked, and the men pulled fish after flapping fish over the sides of their boat with long gaffs. I'd like to say we defended our fish and yelled at the fishermen to leave us alone, or tried to row away from their nets, but we didn't. Caught up in the shock of seeing other people, by the time we thought of doing something, it was too late. Content with their day's catch, the men pulled in their lines and headed back to Martinique.

I peered into the waters under our boat. I didn't see one dorado.

"They didn't get Legend," Colin said.

"How do you know?" I asked, feeling my eyes grow moist.

"I was watching them the entire time. Legend wasn't one of the ones caught," Colin said.

I wasn't convinced. We had last seen Legend the previous day, his giant, sleek body cruising the depths beneath us. And it had been difficult to observe the fishing boat through the waves. They could easily have hauled in Legend without our noticing it.

Suddenly Legend's unmistakable form appeared in the water off my starboard oar. He was the only dorado we saw return after the fishermen left; he stayed with our boat for about an hour. When we came within five kilometres of land, the giant fish descended out of sight. We never saw Legend again.

We could now see the island's palm trees distinctly, but the wind still blew at thirty knots. Colin joined me at the oars and sat in the second rowing station, and we rowed in tandem for the first time since leaving Portugal. It had been more efficient for us to spend longer hours rowing individually. But now, hearing the thunder of exploding waves on shore, we needed to maximize our power in order to navigate the final tricky stretch into the sheltered harbour.

Our speed climbed as the current channelled through the passage between St. Lucia and Martinique. We were rowing due south, at a ninety-degree angle to the current, to create the vector to angle us directly past St. Lucia's northern tip. With tension running high and waves thundering onto volcanic rocks only one hundred metres away from us, we finally rounded the point and slipped into the lee of St. Lucia. The reduced wind and current still pushed against us, and we had to turn suddenly and row with all our strength just to hold our ground. I was thirsty and exhausted, but we couldn't stop for a second. If we lost any distance whatsoever, the force of the currents would increase, and we would be swept away from St. Lucia with no chance of making it back. I looked at the GPS. We were moving at zero knots.

"Harder, harder!" I screamed.

Colin's brown skin was soaked with sweat. We pumped in unison to break the stalemate. Suddenly the digital display flashed 0.1 knots east. Perfect. We struggled and pulled, and finally it moved to 0.2 knots. I felt like I was going to throw up, but we couldn't give up, or our next stop would be Costa Rica. I wanted my margarita. In the distance I could see tourists relaxing on a sandy, golden beach. Our speed began to rise quickly—0.4 knots, and then a few seconds later, 1 knot. We had broken free of the currents! A strong wind still blasted against us, but now we moved steadily forward.

"*Yes!*" Colin screamed.

We didn't have detailed charts for St. Lucia, but fortunately one of our reference books had some information on the island, as well as a small-scale chart. We knew that a sheltered harbour and marina lay on the north end of the eastern shore, and that the island was home to about 150,000 people who spoke English and a French-based Creole. We anticipated easy communication and all the luxuries we dreamed of.

"That must be Pigeon Island!" I said, pointing to the rocky outcrop. "Rodney Bay Marina is just around the corner." I couldn't wait to stop rowing. We'd been paddling at a sprinting pace for almost four hours, and my arms had become quivering spaghetti.

We slid through the narrow opening that led into Rodney Bay's turquoise lagoon. The perpetual rolling waves of the open ocean suddenly ceased; for the first time since departing Lisbon four months earlier, our boat didn't rock. I slowed my pace and marvelled at the tropical paradise. A tin rowboat painted bright blue, red, and orange pulled up beside us. The boat's name, *Marley*, was painted on the side and, judging by its Rastafarian rower, it could only be a tribute to the legendary Bob Marley.

"Ya, maan," he said, drawing out his vowels. He swung his dreadlocks over his shoulder and bobbed his head rhythmically, as if to the beat of a song we couldn't hear. "Where you come from?"

"Portugal."

His eyes widened, and he let out a long whistle. "No waay, maan. All the way in a rowboat! Welcome to our island."

News of our arrival spread, and a few other boats came out to greet us—excited locals in their aluminum boats and yachters with inflatables. We passed our video camera to a young man piloting an open boat with *Sparkle Laundry* emblazoned on the side, and he filmed our final moments rowing to shore. I was overwhelmed by all the boats, noise, people, and cheers; I felt like I was in a trance.

We left our flotilla to pull into a free berth near the customs office. A long-haired man in his late twenties walked quickly down the dock with a bag in his hand. He introduced himself as Jean-Marc.

"I saw you coming," Jean-Marc said in a heavy French accent. "And I thought to myself, 'What would I want if I had just rowed across an ocean?' So I go to the liquor store and get you cold beer."

"Thank you," we said in unison. We couldn't have dreamed of a better welcome.

Colin got off the boat first, climbing unsteadily onto the dock. He had a hard time keeping his balance and grabbed our new friend's shoulder for support.

"This is not easy," Colin said. "My knees feel loose, as though they're going to snap." Colin leaned against Jean-Marc with a beer in his hand, making it easy to misinterpret the cause of his poor balance.

Colin insisted on capturing my first steps on camera, so I savoured the cold beer while he set up the equipment. I couldn't believe how quickly our surroundings had changed. Half an hour earlier, we struggled against winds and waves, prepared to spend another month at sea, and now we had access to all the luxuries of land. Reaching land had been my wish so many times throughout this journey, and I often wondered if that wish would ever come true. Now that we had actually landed, I couldn't get over how dreamlike it seemed.

My first step helped me catch up with reality. The dock rolled beneath my feet like a boat in pitching waters, not a pier in a calm lagoon. I struggled with the conflicting input; my eyes told me that the dock was stationary and that the boat pitched, but my sense of balance relayed a different story. I took several tentative steps and stumbled, catching myself just before I fell. After 118 days on a boat, I had all but forgotten how to walk.

We finished our beers with Jean-Marc and awkwardly made our way to the marine offices to register, but by the time we arrived they were closing. They told us to come back the next day. Everything about this island, including the registration procedures, seemed laid-back.

Rodney Bay, the main marina on St. Lucia, has mooring space for more than two hundred boats, and all the amenities any yachter (or rower) could dream of, including restaurants, a grocery shop, a liquor store, a repair shop, and a marine store. Overwhelmed by choices, we tried to decide which fantasies to fulfill first.

We had dreamed about so many things over the previous few months. The top ten things I wanted to do on land were almost all food-related. I wanted a strawberry margarita, fresh fruit, ice cream, thin-crust pizza loaded with cheese, good coffee, and chocolate. I also wanted a shower, clean clothes, new books, and a Canadian newspaper. Colin's list wasn't that different from mine. He wanted a piña colada, black licorice, Maynard wine gums, fresh fruit, good coffee, ice cream, Thai lemongrass coconut curry, fresh salad, and a Canadian newspaper. A shower and clean clothes did not appear on Colin's wish list. I suspected he rather enjoyed not having to bathe.

We worked with unparallelled dedication to fulfill our wish lists. I couldn't remember ever setting about a task with such enthusiasm. We started at a quaint café that served a cornucopia of ice cream flavours. I finally decided on pistachio, although I pledged to return daily to sample the remaining flavours, and Colin found his favourite, coconut. We had often dreamed of this moment, especially on the days we'd sweated on the oars, with the relentless sun scorching our skin and nothing colder to drink than lukewarm water "It's even better than I imagined," Colin murmured to no one in particular, closing his eyes in ecstasy.

We sat on a wooden beach, silently savouring our ice cream and enraptured by the activity around us. Vacationers strolled hand in hand along the waterfront, yachts motored into and out of their slips, locals sold fruit and straw hats, and shops buzzed with activity. Our surroundings seemed so alien. It was as if we had spent the past four months in a parallel world, and now the two worlds had merged.

After we finished our ice cream cones, we returned to the same café for coffee and reclaimed our seat by the water, delighting in the strong Colombian java. We wanted to explore the area and learn what our surroundings had to offer, but the fifty-metre walk between the café and the park bench was all we could muster. The ground continued to roll under each step we took, and I was exhausted from using leg muscles I'd forgotten I had. We must have looked like a couple of drunk invalids, not like athletes.

That night we had dinner with a Canadian yachter in an adjacent upscale restaurant. We ticked several more items off our wish lists: I ordered a Mediterranean pizza with salad and a margarita, and Colin had a Thai chicken curry and a piña colada. Our first meal on land after a third of a year in a rowboat was divine. We must have made terrible dinner companions; not only had we forgotten the etiquette of small talk after so many months alone, but we were too smitten with our culinary experience to focus on much else.

The next day we continued down our top-ten lists. Soupie from the *Sparkle Laundry* (our volunteer cameraman when we'd first arrived) picked up our dirty clothes and returned them clean and folded. I showered in the marina bathroom—my first time bathing in fresh water in four months—and watched as layers of grime peeled off my body and discoloured the water. I marvelled at the lather the soap and shampoo formed in fresh water and savoured the feeling of being truly clean. What I liked less was trying to comb the knots and mini-dreadlocks out of my wet hair. After pulling out enough hair to create a small shag carpet, I emerged just as clean and neat as my freshly laundered clothes. Colin, too, looked dapper, apart from a persistent dreadlock.

Now that we were scrubbed and well-fed, we focussed on the logistics of preparing for the last leg of our row. This wasn't easy. Our boat had become the local tourist attraction, and a constant stream of interesting people distracted us. Generous people took us out to dinner, gave us money to buy meals, and helped us out. The marina manager waived our moorage fees. A Norwegian family with three young kids in the sailboat moored next to *Ondine* gave us a laptop computer to use for the rest of the journey, and Kevlar matting to fix our broken oar.

We spent most of our days either on the boat or at the nearby Internet café, and all our nights on the boat (the only nearby hotel cost several hundred dollars a night). Our

inability to walk more than a few hundred metres was pro-
hibitive, but I was quite content to remain close to the boat.
I felt uncomfortable and even a little agoraphobic when we
strayed too far. Getting used to the real world again would
take time.

A few days after we arrived, our new lead sponsor, Truestar Health, flew their representative Garie MacIntosh out to
meet us. Garie, a neat man in his mid-twenties, arrived at
the marina with a duffle bag full of goodies, including nutritional supplements to complement our diet for the journey
home. No more worries about scurvy.

As Colin and I checked our e-mails at the nearby Internet
café, we received more good news. Wallace & Carey, a Canadian distribution company that had helped with the first half
of Colin's expedition, offered financial assistance to see us
home, and a few other people made donations. For the first
time, I finally felt at ease with my decision to row across the
Atlantic. The end was drawing close, and we no longer faced
pending bankruptcy. From the beginning, despite all our
plans and preparations, it had felt like we were running a fine
line, both financially and logistically. Now I felt the balance
swing in our favour.

We spent much of our time in St. Lucia cleaning the
boat and restocking it. We had four months of trash to dis-
pose of—mostly food packaging—and several grocery carts
full of freshly purchased food to pack. We ordered charts for
the Caribbean Sea and for Costa Rica, and purchased large,
buoyant fenders to tie to our cabin for extra flotation (if we
capsized, they would help the boat right itself).

The outside of the boat needed to be cleaned, too. I
leaned over its side to scrub a brown stain that had formed

above the water line, and a movement in the murky water caught my attention. I peered into the depths.

"Colin, come here quick!" I yelled.

Colin clambered out of the cabin, where he had been scrubbing the mouldy lockers with bleach. "What is it?"

"I think Ted and Fred followed us into the harbour."

"No, they couldn't have. It's crowded and polluted in here, and they're deep-sea fish," Colin replied.

"Well, what's that, then?" I said, pointing to Ted as he surfaced six inches from my hand.

Colin's mouth hung open. "Wow, I guess they really are staying with us. I wonder if they'll follow us back out to sea."

AFTER TEN DAYS in St. Lucia, we were ready to leave, but the weather wouldn't let us. Six-metre waves and ninety-kilometre-an-hour winds hammered the island. Two local fishing boats actually sank, while most of the yachters huddled safely in the marina waiting for conditions to improve. We followed suit.

St. Lucia is a much better place to wait out foul weather than the open ocean. We explored the nearby beach, which offered a panoramic view of St. Lucia's most famous landmark, the Pitons—twin towers of rock that stretched into the sky. The Pitons formed when lava hardened within two volcanic vents and subsequent erosion removed the surrounding rock, leaving only the two jagged tusks that gave St. Lucia a unique profile. We spent many hours lounging around in the marina coffee shop, reading tourist booklets that detailed the island's history. We learned that the island had switched between British and French control so often that it has been deemed "the Helen of the West Indies" after the mythical

Helen of Troy, the beautiful daughter of Zeus. France and Britain fought fourteen wars for St. Lucia, until finally, the British took complete control in 1814. Then, in 1979, it became an independent Commonwealth Nation.

After two days of waiting, the weather improved, and we embarked on the final leg of our voyage across the Atlantic Ocean.

16

THE FINAL LEG
TO COSTA RICA

W E FOUND LEAVING St. Lucia much different from setting off from Lisbon. Four months before, I had been nervous about my abilities and uncertain what the future would hold. Now I felt more confident and looked forward to this final leg. During our stay in St. Lucia, I had actually begun to miss life on the ocean: the birds, the fish, the simplicity.

Unlike our departure from Lisbon, we didn't have to worry about leaving with the outgoing tide. We knew that the west-flowing currents and wind would sweep us along as soon as we paddled a few kilometres from shore.

At 10:00 AM on February 1, I untied the ropes and Colin lowered the oars. We waved goodbye to about twenty people who'd gathered on the dock to wish us good luck and snap photos. Air horns blasted, and shouts of "Bon voyage!" filled the air. Several dinghies and sailboats trailed us as we left.

This warm send-off reflected the generosity we'd felt throughout our stay on St. Lucia.

Swiftly, we moved away from the island, and the waters transformed from turquoise to a darker blue as the ocean floor dropped away. The waves increased in size, and soon the boat swung wildly back and forth. Oddly, I felt I was home again, back in our world of two.

We had chosen our route to Costa Rica carefully. We wanted to avoid as many coral reefs as possible. These fragile ecosystems can be damaged by even a slight impact; they could also easily lead to a shipwreck for us. Sadly, the rise in ocean temperatures has started to kill the microscopic plants, called zooxanthellae, which have a symbiotic relationship with coral polyps. When the plants die, so do the corals. Most of the coral colonies in the Caribbean have already undergone some bleaching (a term that describes the loss of colour in coral that occurs when the zooxanthellae die). When conditions improve, coral reefs can recover from bleaching, but as ocean temperatures continue to rise and as oceans become more acidic, the reefs may reach a point from which recovery is impossible.

It has been predicted that Australia's Great Barrier Reef—the largest reef, not to mention the largest living organism on Earth, and the only one visible from space—will lose 95 per cent of its living coral by 2050. The 2004 report *Implications of Climate Change for Australia's Great Barrier Reef*, commissioned by the wwf and the Australian government, found that although the Great Barrier Reef is one of the healthiest reefs, rising ocean temperatures are causing the coral to bleach and eventually die.

And things have not improved since the release of that report. On the contrary, 2005 was the most devastating year for Caribbean coral since record-keeping began. In 2008, the IUCN published another weighty report, *Status of Caribbean Coral Reefs after Bleaching and Hurricanes in 2005*, to mark the start of the International Year of the Reef. The year we crossed the ocean, intense hurricanes and record high ocean temperatures devastated huge amounts of Caribbean reefs, killing more than half the corals and severely bleaching between 50 and 95 per cent of colonies in the worst-hit areas. Waves from the storms battered the corals, the storm surges caused flooding, and the associated runoff took pollutants to the coral colonies. The high ocean temperatures that caused extensive bleaching also led to outbreaks of infectious diseases among the coral, such as white plague.

It would have been fascinating to explore the beauty of coral reefs from a diver's perspective. But in a wooden boat, we wanted to stay as far away from them as possible. The marine charts for the Caribbean that we had obtained in St. Lucia helped us plot our route. We planned to head almost directly west, staying several hundred kilometres north of South America. When we cleared the most northern point in South America, the Guajira Peninsula off Colombia, we would angle southwest towards Costa Rica.

Keeping our distance from land was important not only for avoiding the coral reefs. We also wanted to avoid the risk of piracy. The waters near Venezuela and Colombia have a reputation for being less than safe. Travel advisories recommend avoiding all off-the-beaten-track areas of Colombia because of drug trafficking, kidnapping, and guerrilla insurgencies. In St. Lucia, we had heard several stories of yachters who had been pillaged in these waters.

After only a few hours of rowing, land faded from view, and we were again surrounded by endless blue. Our time on St. Lucia seemed to have been a very vivid dream, and now we were back to reality. But readjusting to life on the rowboat after a twelve-day hiatus was not completely seamless. Although we found it much easier psychologically than leaving Lisbon, slight seasickness returned, and our lives were again tainted with lethargy, nausea, and headaches.

"LOOK AT ALL this trash," I said in disgust.

Toys, shoes, bags, and reams of unidentifiable plastic floated on the water in a line three metres wide and many kilometres long. I couldn't see the end of it. We had noticed trash throughout our journey, and I had been surprised and disappointed to see plastic bottles and other debris floating in an otherwise pristine environment. Eventually I became used to seeing flotsam on a regular basis. However, the density of trash had markedly increased since we entered the Caribbean Sea, and nothing prepared me for this. Just within our line of sight there seemed to be enough trash to account for a small city.

Colin glanced at the mess. "It looks like the edge of a giant eddy. That's why the trash has collected in such a straight line."

Sadly, this was just a miniature version of the Great Pacific Garbage Patch, the world's largest garbage site located in a remote area in the Pacific Ocean. There, garbage weighing an estimated three million tonnes covers an area as large as

British Columbia and the Yukon Territories combined. Currents slowly swirl clockwise, drawing garbage in and keeping it there. The same thing was happening here; currents had captured garbage from across the Caribbean.

The Caribbean Sea also suffers from less visible trash. Ninety per cent of sewage dumped into the sea by surrounding countries and ships is untreated. Each year, fifty thousand ships travel these waters, making it one of the busiest waterways in the world. Cruise ships bring many of the region's 14.5 million annual tourists, but resources to monitor and handle waste disposal are limited, and the industry has a poor record of compliance. A significant amount of tanker traffic also travels the Caribbean, and oil spills are a regular problem.

In the water, amidst the trash, I could see Ted and Fred swimming underneath my oars. They had followed us from Rodney Bay Marina, and a few other fish had since joined them. Although Ted and Fred now swam six thousand kilometres away from where they had originally joined our boat, they seemed to be doing just fine. I wondered at their ability to survive in waters so markedly different from their natural habitat. Not only were these waters more polluted, they were warmer and undoubtedly had different predators and food sources.

TWELVE DAYS AFTER leaving St. Lucia, we had rowed 1,100 kilometres and were about to enter an area prone to high winds. Our pilot charts indicated that this anomalous region, 200 kilometres northwest of the Guajira Peninsula, had wind speeds significantly higher than those in surrounding areas and waves two and a half metres or higher more than 40 per cent of the time.

"Maybe we'll get lucky and have pleasant conditions that appear the other 60 per cent of the time," I said, as Colin and I studied the pilot charts.

Colin gave me a dubious look. "If there's a chance of bad weather, we're going to get it."

"What happened to Mr. Optimistic?" I chided.

"I'm optimistic that we'll be able to deal with it even better than before. Our boat is more seaworthy than it's ever been," Colin said.

He glanced up at the inflated plastic fender we had strapped to our roll bar. It would give us extra buoyancy, further assisting the boat's self-righting capabilities. We had also filled all our empty fuel jugs with water to increase our ballast and give us extra stability.

We had passed Venezuela. Colombia lay to our south, its northeastern tip jutting out to funnel and condense the currents flowing along the South American coastline. This three-knot flow was the fastest we had yet experienced, and we made forward progress at incredible speeds exceeding five knots.

I prayed the good conditions would remain. We were approaching Costa Rica faster than anticipated; if the conditions stayed constant, we'd successfully complete our row in another ten days.

APPARENTLY, ENDING OUR journey smoothly was too much to ask for. The storm started on Valentine's Day, a mere eight hundred kilometres away from Limón, Costa Rica. We cancelled our romantic dinner of spaghetti and wine and replaced it with ramen noodles softened in cold water. The weather escalated quickly, with waves quadrupling in size within just a few hours and winds whipping up to more than gale-force speeds. The water frothed too much for us to see Fred, Ted, and the others, but I hoped they would stick with us.

When darkness fell, we discovered the danger of staying on deck. The overcast sky blocked the light from the moon and stars, and we could no longer see the waves that reared up to hit us. Only their mighty roar prepared us for their onslaught. The whole ocean seemed to be grumbling; every moment, we dreaded a potential capsize.

We sought safety inside the cabin, sandwiching ourselves between its padded walls. We lay head to foot, and Colin's toes poked me in the face. I leaned against the heavy life raft canister to pin it into place; two cords securing it had snapped, and now it threatened to career free with every breaking wave. Colin's face pressed against the hatch; on occasion he briefly opened it, and air rushed into the hot, oxygen-deprived cabin. Water dripped from the roof every time a wave hit us, and earlier that day a wave had caught us with our hatch open, drenching everything inside. The interior was wet beyond damp, and the unpleasant, musky odour of mildew, sour milk, and mouldy clothing filled the air.

Our efforts to keep the boat shipshape were failing, and the armies of chaos reigned. We couldn't dry our wet bedding and clothing, so our clothes were rotting. We continually spilled food, and crumbs worked their way into crevices and corners. The disorder continued outside the cabin. All our cooking utensils had been swept into the bilge, along with a flying fish that had mistimed its leap and now rotted amid a malodorous slime. Much to our dismay, salt water found its way into our drinking water container, and conditions were too rough to run the desalinator. The alcohol fuel for our stove had also been diluted by salt water that had seeped through its wick, and it would no longer ignite.

Although rowing was out of the question, we found a way to harness some of Mother Nature's relentless energy. Left on its own, our boat turned sideways to the waves and resisted the forward forces. But by constantly controlling the rudder, we could point the bow downwind. In this way, the boat would quickly accelerate with all the ocean's forces behind it. We took turns sitting in the cockpit and steering the boat with the rudder lines while we moved forward averaging 1.5 knots.

We are surviving the storm, I wrote in my journal. *It feels like a traffic accident repeated over and over. The waves are monsters and they break far too often. The worst is when they break against us or on top of the boat—*Ondine *careens on the foam and white spray shoots up the sides of the boat and behind it in a formation Colin calls "rooster tails." We momentarily lose steering control and the boat surfs down the wave. From inside, it is far less frightening and I can almost pretend that I am someplace else—but outside, that luxury doesn't exist.*

On one breaking wave, we clocked our fastest speed ever as our seven-metre rowboat turned into a giant surfboard. Double rooster tails sprayed up from the sides, and our GPS clocked almost thirteen knots, or about twenty-two kilometres an hour.

After three days the storm began to subside and the swells decreased in power. Dean informed us that the gale was still blowing, but since it was stationary, we had moved through to the other side and into calmer waters. During the storm, I hadn't seen Fred and Ted; I was thrilled to spot them in the water again, wagging their little tails. The boat was a stinking mess, and I felt like a survivor emerging from a disaster zone. But Costa Rica, now only five hundred kilometres away, was becoming a very tangible destination.

EACH TIME ANOTHER storm enveloped us, it reminded me just how fragile and ill-equipped humans are to handle many of nature's challenges. The sea is one of the last wild places untamed by humans, a humbling thought in itself. The arrogance and confidence I once felt—knowing I'm at the top of the food chain, living largely unaffected by the negative forces of weather, starvation, disease, and the multitude of other dangers that animals face—quickly dissipated on this journey. Being in a small boat on a turbid ocean reminds us that the human being is just another mammal that evolved with certain strengths, along with many weaknesses. We don't have a sixth sense like the shark, nor can we see in the dark like the dolphin. We don't have the turtle's hard shell to protect our bodies from danger or the speed to outpace an approaching storm.

Our success as a species is mainly due to a single evolutionary advantage: a hefty brain that has allowed us to flourish despite our many shortcomings and to dominate in a way no other animal has. But just because we can outcompete other species and convert our environment to best suit our needs does not mean we have the right to do so, or that it is in our best long-term interest.

Indeed, our greatest advantage could also be our ultimate downfall for more reasons than just the damage inflicted on our environment. Our brains have separated us from the natural world and changed priorities that hundreds of thousands of years of evolution equipped us for. Richard Louv, author of *Last Child in the Woods*, coined the term "Nature Deficit Disorder" to describe the behavioural problems of children who spend little time outdoors. He proposes nature as a therapy for depression, obesity, and Attention Deficit Disorder, and environment-based learning for developing problem-solving and critical thinking skills.

Without a doubt, there is something satisfying about being immersed in nature, about relying on long-forgotten skills dusty from disuse, and about stripping away many of the distractions that clutter our lives. Nature has the power to change our perspective, to make us reassess what is important.

Five months at sea certainly did that for me. It made me feel connected to the rhythms of the natural world. It made me realize that my existence is inextricably intertwined with the lives of other creatures and that our needs are often not dissimilar.

"YOU CANNOT LAND in Costa Rica," the voice boomed through the satellite phone. "It is against the law."

"We can't go anywhere else," I pleaded. "We are in a rowboat and can't paddle back against the winds."

My words fell on deaf ears. Our third phone call to the Canadian Embassy in Costa Rica had us no closer to being allowed to land than our first two calls. Colin's passport had expired a few days before. When we left Portugal, we had assumed our crossing would take less than four months, and that Colin's passport would still be valid when we reached our destination. At that time we had also been aiming for

Miami, and Canadians did not require passports for entry into the United States.

But things had changed, and it looked like Colin's expired passport might prevent us from completing our Atlantic row. We had contacted the Costa Rican Canadian Embassy, who, in turn, had consulted the Costa Rican immigration authorities on our behalf. Unfortunately, Costa Rica is a very bureaucratic nation; they make few exceptions to their rules. They informed the Canadian Embassy that if Colin arrived without a valid passport, he would be jailed and deported. We tried to explain that we'd come to Costa Rica only because we were blown off course by two hurricanes and two tropical storms, but they remained firm: "You need to get a valid passport before you arrive in our country."

I hung up the phone, dejected.

"What are we going to do?" I asked. "We're less than two hundred kilometres away from Limón—we're going to be there in three or four days whether they like it or not."

"Well, they can't exactly turn us away," Colin said. "Unless they donate a big outboard motor. We'll be rowing on the spot as we try going back against these winds. But I guess they could confiscate the boat and deport us."

"What do you mean, *us?*" I said in mock outrage. "*I* have a valid passport and the boat *is* in my name."

"Will you wait for me?" Colin said, fluttering his eyelashes in a pitiful mockery of feminine persuasion. After that failed to elicit a response, he shrugged his shoulders. "Besides, there's nothing I could have done—I've been on an expedition for the last two years."

"I know, and I'm not blaming you. I just wish we could find someone with the power to help us."

SOMETIMES WISHES DO come true. The Discovery Channel wanted to film our arrival for their television show *Daily Planet*, and they had been in touch with port authorities and the Canadian Embassy to make arrangements. Word soon spread. The government must have decided that shipping Colin off in handcuffs as he reached land was not the image it wanted to broadcast. Instead, Colin would be issued an emergency passport just before he stepped ashore. The Canadian Embassy kindly agreed to assist and promised to send two representatives from the country's capital, San José, to Limón to meet us as we arrived.

With that problem almost resolved, we had just two hundred more kilometres to row. I studied the marine charts while Colin rowed. Although we didn't need to worry about reefs here, our approach would be hampered by strong currents parallelling the land. To combat these southward flows, we decided to voyage northwards of Limón. It was like swimming across a river in which you need to aim upstream of your final destination.

As we closed in on Costa Rica, the skies turned dark and brooding, and an unmarked current began flowing against us. Our speed continued to decrease, and torrential rains began to fall.

"I'm not even doing half a knot," Colin yelled.

I peered through the hatch, out to a gloomy, rainy world. On my shift I had averaged only half a knot, but conditions had since worsened, and Colin was now rowing frantically.

"The winds are against us, too; I don't think we'll be able to make progress much longer going solo," Colin said. "We need to row together."

I joined Colin at the oars and our speed increased to almost one knot. We rowed five nautical miles in five hours. We still had more than fifty nautical miles to Limón.

"I don't know if we can make it," Colin said, echoing my thoughts. "If these currents don't change, we'll die of exhaustion before reaching land."

We were exhausted, and it showed in our eroding pace. We were so close to finishing our journey, but it wouldn't be over until we powered through these countercurrents. At this rate, it would take fifty hours of non-stop tandem rowing to reach shore. I felt like a starving person who could see a plate of food just beyond my reach.

For the next forty-eight hours we rowed non-stop. During the day we rowed in tandem, and at night we took turns, so that each of us could catch a bit of sleep. When we rowed alone, we barely held our ground; only when we rowed in tandem did we move forward. We were miserable. No words were spoken, except for those of sheer necessity.

When a waterspout erupted in the distance, I called Colin out of the cabin. "We'll be fine as long as it doesn't hit us," he said flatly.

A waterspout is a spiralling vortex of water that connects the ocean to a dark blanket of cumuliform clouds. These tornados on the sea suck water and, occasionally, fish and boats, upward at wind speeds of 100 to 360 kilometres per hour. They sometimes take fish up into the clouds, and winds carry the fish until eventually, they fall out of the sky. The United States, Mexico, India, Brazil, and England have documented cases of raining fish (and frogs). Waterspouts can be extremely hazardous to boats, and some say they are responsible for many of the mysterious disappearances in the Bermuda Triangle. We desperately wanted to avoid the waterspout, but as always, our slow movement put us at the mercy of the weather. I continued rowing at a right angle to the swirling vortex and anxiously watched it in the distance until it dissipated several kilometres from our boat.

ON THE OCEAN, the air is largely odourless (we had become desensitized to our own stench), making the slightest change noticeable, and now we noticed something new. A deep, rich smell like freshly overturned earth filled our nostrils and reached the most primal part of our brains. We later learned that heavy rains had just caused massive landslides in Costa Rica. Whether this was what we smelled or not, the powerful, singular scent filled me with longing for terra firma. I wanted to kneel on the earth, to dig my hands into it and bring fistfuls to my face so that I could inhale its distinct aroma. I was ready to return to the world that evolution had equipped me for.

"*It's land!*" Colin yelled.

I turned around, searching for an aberration on the horizon. I saw a thin line of blue sky sandwiched between the low cloud ceiling and the ocean, and in it the shadow of distant land.

As we continued rowing, we realized we were approaching a busy shipping port. We cowered among giant freighters plying the waters around us. The occasional cruise ship, lit up like a colossal Christmas ornament, filled us with a mixture of dread and envy. We kept our VHF radio and flares handy in case of pending collisions and continued rowing uneasily.

Strange, low, choppy waves made tandem rowing difficult, and we found that rowing individually in sprints was faster. One of us rowed intensely for half an hour, as though in an Olympic race, before we quickly swapped spots. By continuing this relentless routine through the night, we travelled against the current at one knot. Torrential rains soaked us to the bone. Rowing quickly warmed us, but our teeth chattered between shifts. Huddling beneath a wet blanket didn't help.

The navigation lights of Limón's port beckoned through a minefield of anchored freighters as we neared shore. The current finally released its hold on our boat.

"We made it," Colin said quietly.

It seemed unreal. I had just completed something momentous, and the next morning we would step onto land. I should have been in a celebratory mood. But the last three and a half days had been the most trying of my life. We had barely eaten or slept. I shivered in the cold. I wanted to vomit. The most exciting thing at the moment was that I could finally rest. We dropped anchor in the shallow waters between moored freighters and fell asleep.

WHEN I OPENED my eyes, it was still dark, but I could smell coffee. Colin was already making breakfast.

"Good morning, Tiger," he said. "How does it feel to have rowed across the Atlantic Ocean?"

"Amazing," I said.

We were scheduled to arrive at the port in two hours. We would be greeted by the Discovery Channel film crew, officials from the Canadian Embassy, customs and immigration authorities, and local media. It would be a dramatic contrast to the solitude of the ocean, and we both needed a bit of time to prepare. As we sipped our coffee, we reminisced about moments at sea and watched our piscine pets swimming beneath us. Fred and Ted were still with us. We recognized Fred from the thin scar that marked his back and Ted by the notch out of his tail. We had named others, too, but Fred and Ted were dearest to us because of all the experiences we shared. They had been with us for most of our ten-thousand-kilometre journey.

"We could take them back to Canada with us," Colin said, half-seriously. "You know, put them in a plastic bag and ship them home."

"I'm going to miss them," I said, knowing that taking them home was impossible.

Fred, Ted, and the other fish had been more than just companions. They had helped sculpt my experience on the ocean. In a way, they had been our guides across the sea. They did not lead the way, but their presence opened my eyes to a world I wanted to understand. So often, when I struggled with my own insecurities and doubts, I peered into the waters at their tiny bodies wiggling furiously to keep pace with us and laughed. They reminded me to pay attention to the here and now, to observe the world instead of getting caught up in a frenzied rush to nowhere. On the ocean, just as in regular life, it is possible to become self-absorbed and lose sight of what's important.

For me, this journey had started twenty years before, when I stared into my aquarium, wishing I could live in a fish's world. This voyage had taken me as close to that child-hood fantasy as I could imagine. When we began, I thought of the ocean as a separate world from the one we live in, but throughout the journey, I discovered just how inter-connected we are. The health of life on land depends on the vitality of the seas, which cover over 70 per cent of our world. Yet, because of our dependency on it and activity in it, we've caused fish stocks to dwindle, turtles to become endangered, and coral reefs to die. It's a very delicate balance, and we need to learn much more about it. We have mapped the moon better than we have the sea floor, and even though we discover hundreds of new ocean-dwelling species each year, an estimated one million or more species remain to be found. It can be hard to cherish something we do not understand.

I joined Colin outside and we slid both pairs of oars into the water. We rowed the final hundred metres of the Atlantic in tandem, not because rough weather required it, but because we wanted to celebrate this event together. During these past six months we had shared an incredible array of experiences. For the rest of our lives, we would reflect on the Christmas we had spent in the middle of the ocean, the hurricanes that had submerged us in five-storey waves, the colossal turtle that had loved our boat almost to death, and the great white shark that had peered up at us from an arm's length away. These moments united us and changed our perspectives. They exposed us in our rawest element and brought us closer together. We began this journey worried about all the things that could go wrong between us, but instead we discovered how to work as a team in even the most dismal conditions. We both knew now, more than ever, we had found the right person to spend our lives with.

EPILOGUE

COLIN AND I spent two weeks in Costa Rica, devouring
fresh fruits and vegetables and spicy Caribbean
dishes. Although we'd completed our Atlantic crossing, we had one last leg to finish—an 8,300-kilometre bicycle journey back to Vancouver. Conveniently, friends flying
to Costa Rica on vacation brought us two lightweight bicycles from home. We arranged to store *Ondine* in a secure
compound in the Port of Limón and prepared to depart.

We pedalled out of Limón considerably plumper than
we'd been on arrival, and made our way through Nicaragua,
El Salvador, Guatemala, Mexico, and the United States and
finally into Canada. After two months of steady cycling, we
reached Vancouver on May 20, 2006. A crowd of cheering
friends and family greeted us; music played, cameras snapped,
and I cried. It was a great homecoming. For Colin, it was the
completion of a long-held dream; he had travelled 43,000
kilometres around the world to complete the first human-

powered circumnavigation. And I was thrilled to have jour-
neyed halfway around the world from Moscow using only a
bicycle and a rowboat.

As Colin and I adjusted to the regular world, people
often asked me if I now found life mundane. Surprisingly, I
didn't find being home boring at all; on the contrary, it was
an adventure of a different sort. On the rowboat we had
dreamed of living in a quiet country home on Vancouver
Island, so when we returned we set about doing just that.
We retrieved our belongings from the storage locker in Vancouver and moved to the beautiful Comox Valley. Colin
finished his book *Beyond the Horizon*, which detailed his circumnavigation and went on to become a national bestseller.
Together we produced an expedition film that won several
film festival awards, including Best Adventure Film at Taos
Mountain Film Festival. We then organized a film tour
that took us from Victoria to Halifax, and spent two months
meeting almost seven thousand Canadians who came to our
presentations.

Perhaps the most rewarding experience has been creating this book. The process has allowed me to reminisce and
revisit a journey that has changed me immeasurably. When I
think back to the Atlantic row now, it has the hazy edges of a
vivid dream; it seems like an experience from another world.
The girl who pulled so hard on those oars and who struggled
against hurricane-force winds seems to be a character other
than myself. But reliving the events in the pages of this book
has added tangibility to my memories.

After surviving tempests in a rowboat, Colin and I felt
quite certain we could weather those of matrimony. So on
August 11, 2007, we were married. Our honeymoon—no

surprise to those who knew us well—was a rowing trip. We designed and built two coastal rowing boats and cavorted around Vancouver Island for ten days. Now we've taken those same boats to Scotland and are in the process of rowing to Aleppo, Syria. Before you point out that Aleppo is not a coastal city, I should mention that the boats are designed to be towed behind a bicycle on land. When we're on water, the bikes and trailers fit into the watertight hatches of our boats. We are travelling on a network of canals, cycling paths, great rivers (Thames, Rhine, and Danube) and several seas, including the Mediterranean, the North Sea, and the Black Sea. As I write these words in May 2008, we are on the Thames River on the outskirts of London, having rowed and cycled here from John o'Groats at the northern tip of Scotland. In a week, we'll cross the English Channel to France, and by October we'll have reached Syria.

ACKNOWLEDGEMENTS

THIS BOOK, AND the adventure, would not have been possible without the time, talent, support, and encouragement of a number of incredible people and companies.

The dedicated staff of Greystone Books guided me through a journey almost as difficult as rowing across the Atlantic Ocean. I'd like to thank Nancy Flight and Rob Sanders for embracing this project and for their invaluable advice in developing the manuscript. I am especially indebted to the talented Susan Folkins, who not only did a magnificent job editing the book, but managed to work with me as I was rowing and cycling across Britain. More than a handful of friends and family members motivated and encouraged me during the writing process; they were also a part of my cheerleading squad during the expedition, so I'll thank them in that context.

While we were on the ocean, we relied on friends for endless support—not only for the occasional heartening word but for relaying weather forecasts, updating our website, transcribing newspaper stories, and a litany of odd requests such as getting two bicycles to Costa Rica or renewing a passport while at sea. Dean Fenwick did all this and more; not only did he become our de facto home-based coordinator, but before we left he ensured our boat and all the equipment we needed arrived in Portugal. His girlfriend, Sarah Evans, now a doctor, provided much appreciated medical advice. More thanks go to Mary Hearnden and Dan Carey, who ensured our life raft and EPIRB arrived in Portugal; Christine Leakey, who supplied us with weather forecasts and connected us with our lead sponsor, Truestar Health; Shelley Russell, for too many reasons to list; Corinne Hockley and her mother Leigh, for hours of transcribing; and many other dear friends, including Jackie and Vance Bellerose, Karen Best, Alex Binkley, Jason Brannon, Dennis Breymann, Liz Cameron, James and Shelley Campbell, Frank and Anita Carey, Cathy Choinicki, the Davies Family, Mario DeAlmeida, Jennifer Hamilton, Brad Hill, KJ and Murray Klonz, Greg Kolodziejzyk, John Tracey Leiweke, David Morgan, Carole Paquette, Bob Pope, Lloyd Pritchard, John Rocha, and Randi Spentzos. This is not, by any means, a complete list; many others have helped in pivotal ways, and even though they are not individually listed I would like to express my gratitude for their kindness.

An expedition of this magnitude is not possible without the support of companies who share our values, and we were lucky to work with a number of outstanding organizations. These include Truestar Health, Wallace & Carey Inc., Helly Hansen, Kelowna Flightcraft, Norco Performance Bikes, Specialized Office Systems, Iridium Satellite Solutions, Vancouver Rowing Club, LiferaftRental.com, Mountain House,

acknowledgements

ChristineLeakey.com, SiteAction.com, KOKO Productions, Rodney Bay Marina, Mountain Equipment Co-op, and Croker Oars Australia.

I need to thank my family the most, for at times, this adventure was undoubtedly more challenging for them than it was for me. I made my mother, Helga Wafaei, worry tremendously, and even though she didn't entirely approve of my adventure, she still loves me unconditionally. The same is true for my father, Husam Wafaei, his wife Lina, and their children Nouri and Yasmeen, who have always been supportive and interested. My now-mother-in-law, Valerie Spentzos, was one of our biggest motivators on the ocean, and she continued her cheerleading while I wrote this book by creating a blooming oasis of dahlias in our garden and by plying me with farmers' market cookies. Indeed, I am lucky to be so warmly embraced by Colin's family; they are all great. His brother, George Spentzos, made our expedition possible by lending us enough money interest-free to purchase our rowboat, and Colin's sisters Patty and Jane Spentzos have been equally enthusiastic.

The person most pivotal to the completion of both journeys is my husband Colin, who knows how much he means to me. I am also extremely grateful to the bus stop that caused our paths to cross.